TORONTO

THEN&NOW

A MAN SITS ALONE WITH A BOOK, THE WHOLE WORLD AROUND HIM GROWS SILENT, A VOICE SO SECRET IT CAN'T BE HEARD, JUST FELT,
IS WHISPERING TO HIM AND LEADING HIM DEEP INTO THE WORLD OF THE GREATEST WONDER AND POWER - HIS OWN IMAGINATION.
MORLEY CALLAGHAN

Aerial view of downtown Toronto looking to the east over Ontario Place and the Canadian National Exhibition.

"*The situation of the town is very unhealthy, for it stands on a piece of low marshy land, which is better calculated for a frog-pond or beaver-meadow than for the residence of human beings.*"

Edward A. Talbot
Five years resident in the Canadas, 1824.

TORONTO, THEN & NOW

By: Mike Filey with Rosalind Tosh
Photography: John McQuarrie

Published by: Magic Light Publishing
                       John McQuarrie Photography
                       192 Bruyere Street
                       Ottawa, Ontario
                       K1N 5E1

                       (613) 241-1833
                       FAX: 241-2085
                       e-mail: mcq@magma.ca

Design: Dave O'Malley and John McQuarrie
Production   Diane Donaldson, Aerographics
Printing: Book Art Inc., Toronto

Canadian Cataloguing in Publication Data

Filey, Mike
 Toronto, then & now

ISBN 1-894673-00-X

1. Toronto (Ont.)–Pictorial works. 2. Toronto (Ont.)–History–Pictorial works. I. Title.

FC3097.37.F524 2000   971.3'541'00222   C00-901027-0
F1059.5.T6843F56 2000

Printed and bound in Hong Kong, China

CONTENTS

Aerial view of the Toronto night sky looking to the west over Yonge Street.

"With imaginative municipal leadership, there might even be some thought of Toronto and its immediate environs functioning as a city-state, a Singapore of the West, but there would be none of the criteria of nationhood."

Conrad Black

INTRODUCTION

ALL CITIES IN THEIR GROWTH AND DEVELOPMENT REFLECT THEIR OWN HISTORIES. IN EACH NEW ERA AS CITIES STRIVE TO RECAST AND REINVENT THEMSELVES TO MEET THE CHALLENGES OF NEW TIMES, NEEDS AND OPPORTUNITIES, THEY REVEAL IMPORTANT ASPECTS OF THEIR ESSENTIAL CIVIC DNA BORN OF THEIR OWN UNIQUE CULTURAL AND NATURAL HERITAGE.

In Toronto, one fundamental recurring theme has been the need to protect, enhance and celebrate the strength of our public realm. Modern Toronto was not established in the 18th century by dint of private aspiration or in response to commercial ambition or to satisfy a need for religious sanctum. It was created as a deliberate act of public policy to serve British Imperial strategies in opposition to the American Revolution. The ensuing colonial administration's requirement for all citizens to maintain "peace, order and good government" and to ensure the general accessibility of the common law gave little York its operative civic code. In consequence, it bequeathed to Toronto a legacy of civic behaviour and city building which has influenced our attitudes and expectations to this day.

This attachment to our public realm as an identifying characteristic has brought us enormous benefits. By insisting at our birth on the practical administrative principles of inclusiveness, accessibility and public order, we have had available to us cultural habits of mind and heart which have allowed us to shape our public places, spaces and services in our own particular way. It is worth noting in passing that these principles also have played a major role in our ability to come closer to meeting the tests of equity and social justice which have become so crucial to our social peace in an increasingly diverse city. A second recurring theme has been our particular approach to economic and social change. We have always understood the importance of economic growth to Toronto's future. We know that it's the main reason people come here and why they stay - better prospects for themselves and their families. Moreover, successive waves of human migration and constant changes in our economic possibilities have taught us to appreciate the power of individual initiative and private endeavour to create wealth.

However, perhaps out of our general sense of community or the legacy of our attachment to the public realm, we have always required an over-arching frame of reference - a publicly understood and accepted context for change - a shared sense of the "big picture" before major public and private investments for change can take place.

"Progress" was the accepted context for change in the railway building era of 19th century Toronto. "Progress" meant industry and industry meant the railroads. We changed our place making and land use ideas to suit the new economy. In the process, we transformed a colonial town into an industrial city which drew people and industries from all over the world. We created a sense of energy and urgency, welcomed new ideas and established a formula for success which has benefited Torontonians for decades.

We pursued a similar path in the aftermath of a deep depression and two world wars in the first half of the 20th century. "Growth" was our goal - our newly rekindled context and frame of reference for the future. We wanted to make sure we were part of the new expanding consumer economy. In order to do so we burst out of our old boundaries to create "suburbia", constructed subways and expressways and built high-rises. We wanted what was "new" and discounted what was "old" and tried to ensure through "education" the equality of opportunity which we felt was central to our civic inheritance and crucial to our future success. We absorbed people from all around the world and transformed our social base. We retooled and expanded our economic strengths and reorganized our government to give it a regional metropolitan context. We knew this would allow for massive investments in both our public and private sectors and thereby change forever the old industrial Queen City and firmly establish the new metropolis of Toronto.

In the later third of the 20th century we insisted on a more balanced understanding of growth, one which would include the importance of neighbourhoods to the health of the city; the livability of downtown and a greener Toronto. We became known in the eyes of many around the world as "the city that works".

By the beginning of the 21st century, tiny York, colonial Toronto, the industrial Queen City and the metropolis of the 20th century, has been transformed into an exploding global city region of some 5 million people. And once again we have embarked on our historic process -

The large warehouse in the center of the archival photo, now known as the 'Queens Quay Terminal', is visible in the large colour photograph just to the left of the page break. This contemporary aerial view is looking to the north west and reflects the development of Toronto's downtown waterfront area in a half century.

Aerial view of waterfront looking to the north east, c. 1950.

Aerial view of waterfront looking to the north west.

the need to reinvest in our public realm and to search for a "new" set of organizing ideas publicly understood and agreed upon which will allow public and private initiatives to move forward.

The city government in response to our new challenges, has launched a process of public discussion to discover these new organizing ideas. In a splendid report, Toronto at the Crossroads: Shaping our Future, they have articulated five Campaigns of Action:

Campaign for Beautiful Places
Campaign for Next Generation Transportation
Campaign for a Green Toronto
Campaign To Make Housing Happen
Campaign for a Dynamic Downtown

Sound familiar? It should. These themes have been with us since the beginning.

Nowhere is this more true than on Toronto's waterfront. The waterfront is a special place. It's where nature meets culture and where Toronto was born. From earliest times, long before the coming of the French and English and muddy York, deep in the mists of aboriginal time, Toronto was a meeting place for trade and commerce and festivals, sustained by continuing community and sanctified as a holy place.

With magnificent valleys reaching down from the Oak Ridges Moraine to the lake, cradling a network of creeks, streams and rivers, the waterfront is the most dramatic topographical feature of Toronto.

Because it is so crucial to our economic, environmental and social well-being, the waterfront has been singled out for special treatment throughout our history. In the early colonial days it was not only vital for commerce, trade, transportation and defence, it was also a social and esthetic show piece - a promenade for strolling Georgian and Victorian Torontonians.

In the railway era, it became predominently, a complex web of steel rails going hither and yon across the country and the continent, carrying people and goods to and from the growing industrial city.

In the 20th century, the waterfront and its islands became the target of a number of comprehensive plans which, in their time, dramatically altered the shoreline and transformed its function and uses. The 1912 Plan and the establishment of the Toronto Harbour Commission to implement it came following years of public discussion. Over the decades of its implementation, the basic character of Toronto's modern waterfront was established providing a context for building and development which reflected Toronto's quest for greater industrial and commercial strength and the city's historic desire to use the waterfront for sport, recreation, and boardwalk promenades.

The 1968 50 mile Waterfront Plan, implemented over the years by the excellent work of the Conservation Authority, contributed much to the public realm and laid the basis for an extraordinary "greening" which we have only in the last few years begun to appreciate. This was complimented at that time by the building of Ontario Place by the Provincial government. Also in the 1970s and 1980s, the federal government through the Harbourfront Corporation laid out a bold plan for the central waterfront which reintroduced the idea of significant residential use and established a reputation for accessibility to recreation and the arts. And in the 1990s, the Waterfront Regeneration Trust, with a number of growing activists and community groups, turned to the task of reclaiming the environmental integrity of the waterfront, advocating an integrated approach to economic, ecological and community development along its shores and up its rivers and watersheds.

In the early months of the new century, all three levels of government together spawned a Waterfront Revitalization Task Force which has built on the work of the previous decade and presented to the public a comprehensive vision for change. Out of the ensuing discussions, we will once again work toward publicly agreed upon plans which will strengthen our public realm and establish a context for both public and private investment and development in the 21st century.

The waterfront will certainly look different in 25 years - as will the rest of the City. I think we'll be pleased with the result - especially if we are wise enough to employ the ideas and principles that have served us so well up to now.

Toronto Then & Now provides us with an excellent opportunity to remind ourselves of the richness of that heritage.

David Crombie

DAVID CROMBIE

David Crombie is a former Mayor of Toronto and Member of Parliament. He has also served as Federal Cabinet Minister and as Chancellor of Ryerson Polytechnic University in Toronto. He is the Founding Chair of the Waterfront Regeneration Trust, Chair of the Toronto Heritage Foundation and President of David Crombie & Associates Inc.

Night-time view of the skyline from Centre Island. The Royal York can just be seen to the right of the spine and the original Bank of Commerce building is hidden amidst the newer cluster of bank towers on the right-hand page.

Toronto in 1842, 1906
[from an original drawing by James Cane]
Frederick S. Challener (1869-1959) (not Challenger)
Oil on canvas, 121.9 x 304.8 cm.
City of Toronto Art Collection

IN THE BEGINNING

TWENTY-FOUR BRASS KETTLES, TWO DOZEN HATS, TEN DOZEN MIRRORS, A BALE OF FLOWERED FLANNEL, 96 GALLONS OF RUM, 200 GUN FLINTS AND A SMALL AMOUNT OF CASH. THAT WAS THE PRICE PAID BY THE CROWN TO THE MISSISSAUGA INDIANS IN 1787 FOR THE ONE THOUSAND SQUARE KILOMETRES (386 SQUARE MILES) BORDERING LAKE ONTARIO THAT TODAY ARE HOME TO THE CITY OF TORONTO. MERE TRIFLES, IN EXCHANGE FOR THE ENGINE THAT NOW ENERGIZES THE ECONOMY AND IN LARGE MEASURE DETERMINES THE DESTINY OF THE SECOND LARGEST COUNTRY IN THE WORLD.

Toronto was not Lieutenant Governor John Graves Simcoe's choice for the capital of the newly created Province of Upper Canada. It was first and foremost to be the site of a naval shipyard. His first choice for the new capital was Newark (Niagara-on-the-Lake) until he got there and realized its vulnerability to invasion by the United States. Next he selected the forks of the River Thames, site today of the city that bears the name of the capital of Great Britain, but this choice was vetoed by the Crown. Disappointed, he settled on Toronto as a "temporary" location and in 1793 began construction of a garrison fort and laid out a ten-block town site to the east on lands surveyed for that purpose five years earlier.

This would not be the first European settlement on the site. One hundred and five years after Étienne Brûlé became the first white man to visit the spot in 1615 (23-year-old Brûlé had been left in the New World by explorer Samuel de Champlain in exchange for a Huron who was taken back to France), the French built several trading posts in the Toronto area, the one on the waterfront, which was known as Fort Rouillé and later as Fort Toronto, lasted until 1759. As Simcoe would later do, they had chosen this location partly because of the protective arm of sandy peninsula that curved some nine kilometres (five-and-a-half miles) into Lake Ontario from the mainland to form a natural and defendable safe harbour between the lake and the mainland.

Upper Canada's legislative assembly moved permanently from Newark to its new home in Toronto in 1797, and by 1800 Government House and other newly constructed public buildings were lending an aura of dignity and authority to the greenhorn community. To reflect British dominion, the town carried the name of York, a name change that did not sit well with all people. "Newark, Kingston (and) York are poor substitutes for the original names of the respective places Niagara, Cataraqui and Toronto," lamented British traveller Isaac Weld in 1799. And so, as early as 1804, petitions were made to the Legislature of Upper Canada to restore the original name. In 1834, "Toronto" ascended once more, never to be obscured again.

Bird's eye view of Toronto looking west along Front Street in 1854.
This beautiful painting shows how the waters of Toronto Bay actually
lapped at the back of the South St. Lawrence Market building and how
Front Street followed the original shoreline.
Painting by Edwin Whitefield, City of Toronto Archives.

Today, Toronto is North America's fifth largest city, with one-third of Canada's population living within 160 kilometres (100 miles) of its boundaries and one-half of the population of the U.S. within a one-day drive. The cosmopolitan metropolis is a lot more than "Two million people living in a forest," as one impressed airborne visitor was heard to rave. It is also the "Best global city for business," according to Fortune magazine. "Worldly, wealthy, personable, and relatively problem- free," echoes National Geographic. "Toronto is New York run by the Swiss," enthuses actor and bon vivant Peter Ustinov. But perhaps Art Gallery magazine says it best: "(Toronto is) possibly the most civilized metropolis in the Western Hemisphere."

"Toronto…a kind of New York operated by the Swiss."

Peter Ustinov 1987

"If I were a traveller out of a Black Hole somewhere and had time only for a single metropolis before the rocket left again, I think I might well choose for my inspection the city of Toronto. There is no pretending that it is the most beautiful of towns… It has hardly acquired the rich patina of antiquity, but in the last decades of the twentieth century it has become in many ways a microcosm of its time."

Jan Morris
Renowned Anglo-Welsh travel writer.

FORT YORK

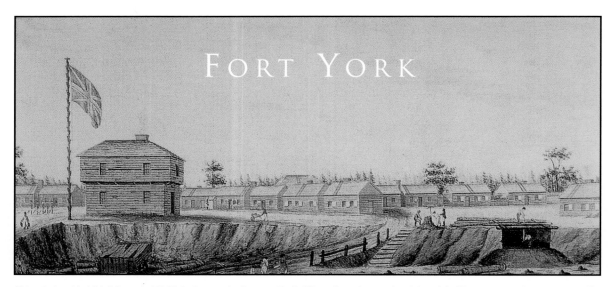

This painting titled "York Barracks, 1804" is by Sempronius Stretton. The buildings shown here replaced the original fort structures that were erected by Governor Simcoe soon after he arrived at the future site of Toronto in 1793. The buildings in this painting were either torn dow or fell down to be replaced by many of those that make up the present Fort York. The fort is the birthplace of Toronto and the most historic site in the entire city.

Tensions did not completely disappear with the end of the War of 1812. Ongoing concerns over possible attacks on the government by dissidents resulted in the construction of several military outposts around the small city such as this one in the forest northeast of Toronto located near present-day Bloor and Sherbourne.

IT IS NOT BECAUSE OF ENEMY ATTACK OR THE RAVAGES OF FIRE, NOR EVEN BECAUSE OF THE PASSAGE OF MORE THAN TWO CENTURIES, THAT THE ORIGINAL 1790S LOG BUILDINGS OF FORT YORK NO LONGER EXIST. RATHER THEY SIMPLY DISINTEGRATED WITHIN FIVE YEARS OF CONSTRUCTION. THE RESOURCES THAT JOHN GRAVES SIMCOE NEEDED TO BUILD A TRULY DEFENDABLE FORT HAD BEEN SENT INSTEAD TO KINGSTON, 250 KILOMETRES (155 MILES) TO THE EAST, A COMMUNITY THE CROWN FELT WAS MORE STRATEGIC, SERVING AS IT DID TO DEFEND THE ST. LAWRENCE RIVER COMMUNICATIONS LINK BETWEEN UPPER AND LOWER CANADA.

Having faced the Americans in their battle for independence less than two decades earlier, Simcoe knew the importance of protecting the capital of Upper Canada from its neighbour to the south who, he believed, would not be satisfied until all of North America was free from British control. And so the disintegrating fort was rebuilt 100 metres (325 feet) east of the original, its cannon facing south to cover the only entrance to Toronto Bay. A blockhouse over on the peninsula in the bay was also erected with north-facing guns to defend the same channel. The fort was further fortified in 1811 by Major-General Isaac Brock because of deteriorating relations between Britain and the U.S. – just in time for the commencement of the War of 1812. Its west wall and circular battery date from this period.

Fort York staff in period uniforms giving a demonstration of military rifle drill.

Nearly a year after war began, a combined force of American army and navy personnel attacked Fort York. With four times the number of men and seven times the number of cannon, an outcome in favour of the invaders was predictable. However, their losses in the six-hour battle were more than double those of the First Nations, British and Canadian defenders combined and included Brigadier General Zebulon Pike, of Pike's Peak fame. The Americans occupied York for six days, looting and pillaging. They removed the Assembly Mace, a revered symbol of legislative authority, and some rare books from the library. The mace was later returned by President Theodore Roosevelt during Toronto's centennial celebrations in 1934. The books, however, are still overdue.

Before departing, the invaders also burned the Parliament Buildings and Government House to the ground. That action triggered the retaliatory burning of the Capitol and President's Mansion in Washington the following year by British troops, after which local citizens rushed to cover the mansion's charred wood with a covering of whitewash – hence the structure's now familiar title of The White House.

American forces invaded York a second time in 1813, unopposed, but a third attempt the following year was repelled by cannon fire from the fort's reconstructed defenses. By the end of the war in late 1814, 18 buildings stood within its walls, and batteries mounting heavy cannon controlled the harbour. A new brick barracks housed up to 100 people – not only soldiers, but also their wives and their children. It's a safe bet, however, that they did not know they were often sitting on top of a fortune. Two vaults in the cellar of the officers' barracks were secretly used to store government and bank monies during the period of instability following the Upper Canada Rebellion of 1837.

Fort York from the air today. The busy Gardiner Expressway is visible to the left, the CN rail corridor to the right.

Concerned about another attack on the city from south of the border, a more substantial "New Fort" was constructed further to the west, but still on the water's edge, in 1841. The water behind the concrete headwall in the foreground of the bottom photo would eventually be filled in and become the location of today's Lake Shore Boulevard and Coronation Park. Over the years Stanley Barracks, as the New Fort came to be known, was slowly encircled by buildings of the Canadian National Exhibition. Today, only the former Officers' Quarters (above) still stands in the middle of a parking lot, its ultimate fate unknown.

Aerial view to the northeast over Stanley Barracks and the CNE towards Fort York, c.1949.

17

The harbour defences at Fort York were maintained only until its cannon and earthworks became obsolete in the 1880s. After that, the fort continued to be used by the military for training, barracks, offices and storage until the 1930s, at which point the city stepped in and readied the site for its largest invasion ever. The onslaught began on Victoria Day 1934, Toronto's Centennial Year, and has not stopped ever since as thousands of residents and tourists each year swarm to the city's most important National Historic Site whose fortified walls encompass Canada's largest collection of original War of 1812 buildings.

Troops parade at Stanley Barracks 1944.

A turn-of-the-20th-century garden party on the lawn in front of Stanley Barracks.

Aerial views looking east along the Lake Shore in the 1940s and today. If you look closely, both Fort York and Stanley Barracks can be found in these two photos. And both the number of buildings lost in Stanley Barracks and the extent of the land reclamation accomplished around the Lakeshore and Coronation Park becomes more evident from these elevated vantage points.

The Toronto Skyline c.1956 and today. For many years the majestic Royal York Hotel and soaring Bank of Commerce building were the two dominant features of the Toronto skyline while the only structures standing on the south side of Queen's Quay were the unimpressive looking transit sheds of Canada Steamship Lines. Nearly a half century later, the sheds have been replaced by waterfront condominiums (bigger perhaps but still unimpressive) while further inland, the sky is pierced by a collection of bank towers. But look closer. See what's still there? The good old Royal York Hotel and the Bank of Commerce.

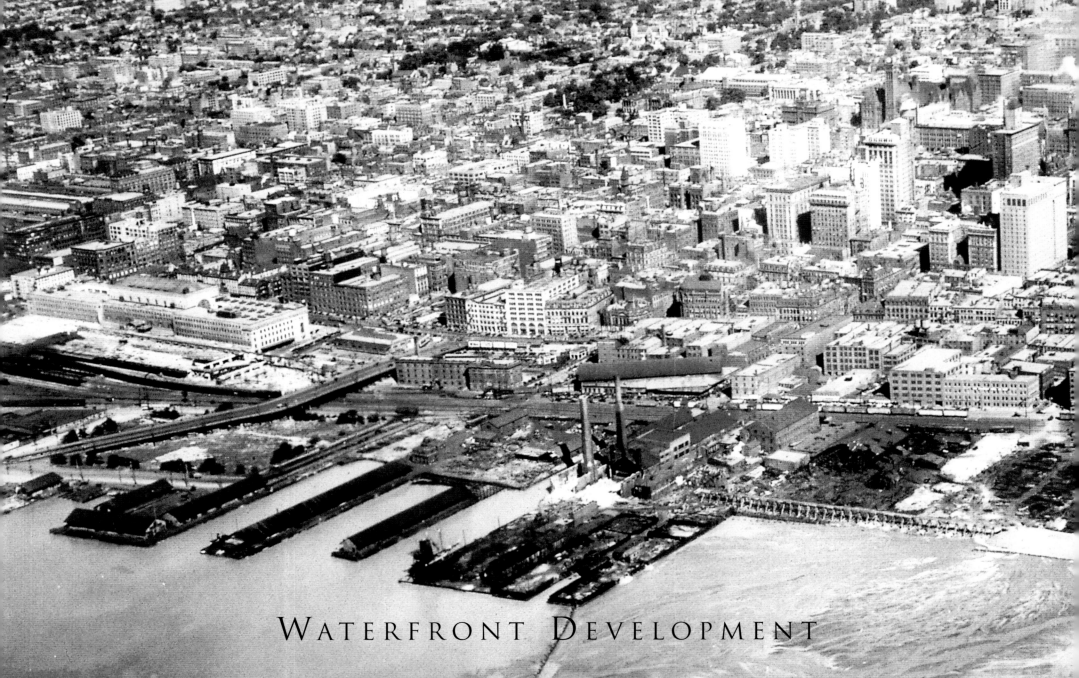

WATERFRONT DEVELOPMENT

INCREDIBLE AS IT SEEMS, THE TENS-OF-HUNDREDS OF TOWERING BUILDINGS, RESIDENTIAL UNITS, FACTORIES, HOTELS, SPORTS FACILITIES, TRANSPORTATION AND COMMUNICATION CENTRES, RESTAURANTS, SHOPS, MUSEUMS, THEATRES, PARKS AND OTHER ASSORTED FEATURES WHICH DOT THE TORONTO WATERFRONT ON THE ACREAGE SOUTH OF FRONT STREET BETWEEN BATHURST AND PARLIAMENT STREETS ARE ALL BUILT ON LAND THAT WAS NOT THERE JUST EIGHT SHORT DECADES AGO. UNTIL 1920, FRONT STREET, NOW MORE THAN 500 METRES (ONE-THIRD OF A MILE) BACK FROM THE LAKE, WAS THE THOROUGHFARE THAT SKIRTED THE WATERS OF TORONTO BAY.

The idea of filling in the bay began in the 1800s. Indeed, if controls had not been established back then, there's a very good possibility that there would be no bay left today, as 19th century entrepreneurs competed for attention by building ever larger piers out into the bay – just as 20th century capitalists were to construct taller and taller buildings. To prevent these wharves and piers being extended until they reached the Island, the Windmill Line bylaw was enacted, drawing an imaginary line over the waters of the bay beyond which no structure could project. The bylaw got its name from the structure which anchored the eastern end of the "line," the windmill at the Gooderham and Worts distillery at the mouth of the Don River. The western end was located at the site of the old French trading post near the present day Bandshell in the Canadian National Exhibition grounds.

"It couldn't be any worse. You can't imagine it. I'm not going to describe it."

Ernest Hemingway 1923
The Toronto Star gave a young Hemingway one of his first jobs as a cub reporter. It appears that the Toronto of the 1920s did not greatly impress the future author.

In this early 1920s concept for what was then known as the "Union Terminal Proposal" we note that today's city officials were not the first to entertain grand hopes for what was possible.

In this contemporary aerial view, again to the north west, we see that while the Union Terminal never materialized, 75 years have borne witness to more than a few changes in the urban landscape.

This 1927 aerial view looking to the north west reflects a city whose waterfront is entirely devoted to shipping and commerce.

Aerial view of the waterfront in 1949 shows the considerable changes that were accomplished in the two preceding decades.

Aerial view of the waterfront in 1969, a mere 20 years after the photograph at left was taken. Canada Steamships is gone, the famous WWII destroyer, HMCS Haida, occupies her temporary berth at the foot of Bay Street, and the Toronto Dominion Centre points to the future of bank tower development.

A scant four years have passed and the year is 1973. New ferry docks, the Harbour Square and Toronto Star buildings have occupied the space of the old warehouses, the Commerce Court has joined the race to be the tallest building downtown and the Royal York and Bank of Commerce buildings have had a face cleaning.

This contemporary view reflects the building boom and economic growth of the last quarter of the 20th century. Many of these wonderful archival aerial views are from the Northway Collection now safely ensconced at the Archives of Ontario. Originally, they appeared in a publication entitled; "Boomtown" - an apt choice of title.

Nevertheless, the problem of an out-of-control waterfront still plagued the city as more and more wharves appeared, some well built, others less so. Finally, in 1911, the newly established Toronto Harbour Commission (reamed the Toronto Port Authority in 1998) was created to bring some order to the chaos. Their $19 million scheme would change the entire city waterfront, from the Humber River in the west to Victoria Park Avenue in the east.

The western lands were allocated for recreation purposes. Aquatic club facilities, a new bathing beach (requiring thousands of cubic feet of clean fill from Pickering Township) and an adjacent amusement park were created, and on June 28, 1922, Sunnyside Beach and Amusement Park was officially opened, to the delight of an eager public. In the east, additional recreational facilities would also be developed, though not nearly so grand in character as those in the west. Additional work was also done to enlarge and improve picnic areas and bathing facilities on Toronto Island.

Between the eastern and western extremities of the city's waterfront lay an area dubbed the Central Waterfront District, consisting of two sectors. The first, in and around Ashbridge's Bay, was developed as the Toronto Harbour Industrial District and became home to many of the city's heavy industries for close to 80 years. Now undergoing transforming rehabilitation and renamed The Port Lands, it will be on these lands – should the city's bid be successful – that the 2008 Olympic Games will be held.

The second sector of the Central Waterfront District underwent perhaps the most profound changes of all. Concrete headwalls were constructed 1100 feet (335.3 metres) out in the bay, parallel to the shoreline between Bathurst Street and Parliament Street, and then these waterlots were filled in. This didn't happen overnight, however. There were some extremely complicated land ownership problems that took until 1929 to resolve and land reclamation in the area continued well into the 1950s. Nevertheless, Toronto's new waterfront was finally created – a landscape that, like the shoreline of the old Island of Hiawatha, is still and forever evolving.

HARBOUR COMMISSION BUILDING

THE PHOTOGRAPHS ON THESE TWO PAGES UTILIZE THE HARBOUR COMMISSION BUILDING AS A VISUAL ANCHOR TO SHOW JUST HOW MUCH LAND WAS RECLAIMED FROM TORONTO BAY. PERHAPS THE MOST REMARKABLE IMAGE IS THE ONE ABOVE WHICH SHOWS THE BUILDING SITTING BETWEEN TWO STEAMSHIP WAREHOUSES, WHICH OCCUPY LAND RECLAIMED FROM THE BAY. BELOW RIGHT WE SEE A 1919 NEWS PHOTO OF A CAPTURED GERMAN U BOAT MOORED DIRECTLY IN FRONT OF THE HARBOUR COMMISSION BUILDING. THE SMALL SAIL BOAT BELOW IS CRUISING PAST RETAINING WALLS WHICH INDICATE THE EXTENT OF THE NEW LANDFILL ABOUT TO COME.

"The entire history of automobiles, airplanes, antibiotics, oral contraception, nuclear energy, computers, plastics, satellites and xerography is encompassed by the span of a single human life."

David Suzuki

By 1949 (above), it is no longer possible to cast your line into the bay from the building's front steps as the venerable old landmark is now completely landlocked. In the contemporary view below the venerable old building can just be seen at center right while, in the aerial image at right, it is hiding in the top-center area.

In this 1973 photograph, a still incomplete CN Tower looms over the warehouses and piers that were part of the original Harbourfront.

HARBOURFRONT CENTRE

ORIGINALLY KNOWN AS HARBOURFRONT, THIS MAJOR WATERFRONT ATTRACTION BEGAN LIFE AS NOTHING MORE THAN A COLLECTION OF EMPTY WAREHOUSES AND INFREQUENTLY USED PIERS THAT STRETCHED ALONG THE CITY'S INNER WATERFRONT FROM YORK STREET ON THE EAST TO STADIUM ROAD ON THE WEST. IN 1972 THE FEDERAL GOVERNMENT PRESENTED THE 40 HECTARE (100 ACRE) SITE TO THE CITY AND IN 1974 HARBOURFRONT WAS BORN. IT WAS DOWNSIZED TO A MORE COMPACT FOUR HECTARE (10 ACRE) SITE IN 1991 WITH A CORRESPONDING NAME CHANGE TO THE PRESENT HARBOURFRONT CENTRE.

The Centre is an innovative, non-profit cultural organization which creates, for a diverse public, events and activities of excellence that enliven, educate and entertain. Working in partnership with various communities, Harbourfront Centre supports educational and recreational activity as well as contemporary artistic creation through showcasing Canadian and international talent.

Young girl enjoying her ice cream cone as she follows the progress of a radio-controlled model of a Canadian Navy frigate.

Man enjoying his morning coffee and his copy of Maclean's magazine on the deck of his antique yacht in the early-morning tranquillity of his Harbourfront slip.

Harbourfront Centre covers 4 hectares (10 acres) from the York Street slip on the east (adjacent to the beautifully restored Queen's Quay Terminal) to the Amsterdam Bridge over the Simcoe Street slip to the west.

The Amsterdam Bridge, named in honour of one of Toronto's twin cities, connects Harbourfront Centre with the old Pier 4, now known as John Quay.

On the John Quay, the Pier 4 Storehouse restaurant (left) and The Pier (right), a museum devoted to the history of Toronto's waterfront, are located in an old warehouse constructed during the Great Depression as a "make work project".

Another view of Pier 4 Storehouse restaurant.

THEATRE

As Toronto finally began to shake off its Victorian manner and enjoy itself. The city's first cocktail bars opened in the late 1940s, Sunday sports were played for the first time, legally, in 1950 and in 1961 going to the movies on Sunday became lawful. In the 1960s there were only two professional live theatres in the city. Today, an eager public is treated to a choice of more than 200 theatre and dance companies performing on over 40 stages and only New York and London sell more English-language theatre tickets in a year.

In the heart of the Toronto theatre district is the Royal Alexandra Theatre which has the distinction of being the oldest continuously operating theatre in Canada and among the oldest in North America, thanks to bargain store owner Ed Mirvish. In 1962, colourful "Honest Ed" saved the theatre from demolition and restored it to its original 1907 beauty, although, as he admitted, he understood little about the arts. But he did know about bargains. "I knew they paid $750,000 to build that theatre," he says. "And I was able to buy it for $215,000, including the land." The 1500-seat Royal Alex was pronounced a National Historic Monument in 1987 and, thanks to Mirvish, is never dark, hosting West End, Broadway and other successful shows 52 weeks a year.

Originally housed at the Royal Alex, the National Ballet of Canada and the Canadian Opera Company moved to the Hummingbird Centre, formerly known as the O'Keefe Centre, when that 3100-seat theatre opened in 1960. Now more than half a kilometre (one-third of a mile) from Lake Ontario, the lands that accommodate the theatre today were, in 1866, smack dab at the water's edge. Where today genteel patrons of the arts sedately seat themselves for an evening's entertainment, back then, the site bustled with travellers and fishermen coming and going from the busy Yonge Street Wharf and neighbouring railway station.

Theatre-goers arriving at the Princess of Wales Theatre on King Street West for an evening performance of the immensely popular "The Lion King".

Elgin and Winter Garden Theatre Centre on Yonge Street under watchful eye of Alfred Hitchcock.

This remarkable pair of playhouses in downtown Toronto comprise the world's only fully restored roofgarden theatre complex and one of the last double-deck theatres found anywhere in the world. The lower theatre, originally known as Loew's Yonge Street, opened in late 1913 and was the Canadian flagship of Marcus Loew's vast chain of vaudeville houses. Just two months later, and high atop the 2,000-seat main floor theatre, the unique Winter Garden opened its doors to the public.

The Princess of Wales Theatre is a new, 2000-seat playhouse built by the father and son producing team of David and Ed Mirvish, The Princess of Wales is the first privately owned and financed theatre built in Canada since 1907 - and the first anywhere in North America in over 30 years. Construction began on August 6, 1991, and the building opened to the public with the musical Miss Saigon on May 26, 1993.

Located only a block apart, on downtown King St. West, the Royal Alexandra and Princess of Wales form the heart of Toronto's "Entertainment District", an area including the city's finest hotels and restaurants and only steps from such major attractions as the CN Tower, SkyDome and the Metro Toronto Convention Centre.

MASSEY HALL

WHEN TYPHOID FEVER CLAIMED THE LIFE OF CHARLES ALBERT MASSEY, HE WAS ONLY 35. SIX YEARS LATER, IN 1890, HE WAS JOINED IN UNTIMELY DEATH BY HIS 24-YEAR-OLD BROTHER, FRED. IN AN EFFORT TO KEEP ALIVE THE MEMORIES OF HIS ELDEST AND YOUNGEST SONS, THEIR GRIEVING FATHER, HART MASSEY — HEAD OF THE LARGEST PRODUCER OF AGRICULTURAL IMPLEMENTS IN THE BRITISH EMPIRE, THE MASSEY MANUFACTURING COMPANY WAS DETERMINED TO HONOUR HIS SONS' PASSION FOR MUSIC AND THE ARTS BY GIVING THE CITIZENS OF TORONTO A NEW CULTURAL CENTRE IN THEIR NAME.

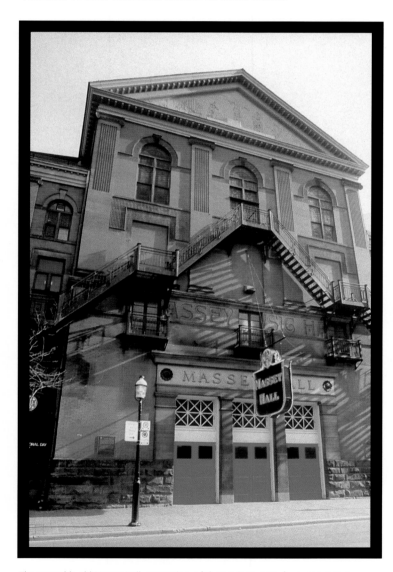

The venerable old Massey Hall, centerpiece of theatre in Toronto for over a century.

It wasn't long before critics attacked the concept, demanding that Massey come up with a "better" idea such as an Agricultural Hall, since he had made his fortune through the farmers of the country rather than its city folk. Other suggestions included a Turkish bath, greenhouses and a park, or poorhouses for the "downtrodden Massey employees." Even the city fathers had no use for the proposal, refusing to grant exemption from municipal taxes. Undaunted, Massey pressed on, and on September 21, 1893, the cornerstone for the new music hall was laid by his six-year-old grandson, Vincent, who 59 years later would begin a seven-year term as the nation's first Canadian-born Governor General.

Just nine months after young Vincent tapped the stone into place, the 3500-seat Massey Music Hall opened with a spectacular three-day music festival, "the finest the public had ever seen," according to the editor of one city newspaper. And Hart Massey was content that his once-unwelcome gift to the people of Toronto was indeed the perfect memorial to his sons — at a price of exactly $152,390.75.

Over the years, the character and intimacy (reduced to 2765 seats in 1933) of Massey Hall has lured the world's superstars, Pavlova, Toscanini, Gershwin, Peterson, Gould, Gillespie, Dylan, Lightfoot, Pavarotti, Callas, Richards. Once, in 1901, opera diva Emma Calvi was interrupted mid-aria as the orchestra abruptly switched to "God Save the King" upon the belated arrival of the future King George V and Queen Mary. And in 1920, just one year before his death, Enrico Caruso gave an unforgettable performance from the top of the fire escape, to the delight of the crowd on the street who couldn't get inside to hear him.

The word "Music" was dropped from the popular venue's name in 1933 to better indicate the breadth of the entertainment being offered. Indeed, music was not the only diversion presented at Massey Hall. In 1908, the world's premier marathon champion, Tom Longboat, chose to be married onstage. Then there was World Heavyweight Champion Jack Dempsey, who in 1919 went a round or two for enthusiastic fans of pugilism. More recently, the Dalai Lama has used the famed acoustics of the "Grand Old Lady of Shuter Street" to spread his message of peace. And those acoustics are indeed first-rate. It is said that listening from the farthest balcony seat in this officially designated Heritage Building is as good as being seated onstage – a claim obviously backed by the Canadian Music Industry which has repeatedly voted Massey Hall Canada's "best live music venue over 1500 seats."

Upper Canada College, northwest corner of King and Simcoe streets, c1895.

THE FOUR NATIONS CORNER

Government House, southwest corner, c.1900.

British Hotel and Tavern, northeast corner, 1908.

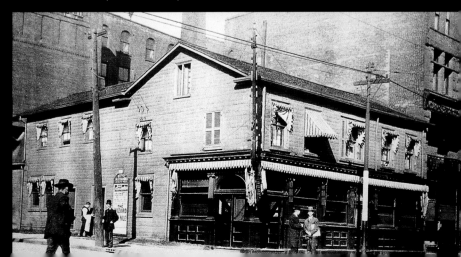

View from Metro Square looking east to the King and Simcoe corner today. St. Andrew's Church to extreme right of photo.

DURING THE LATTER PART OF THE 19TH CENTURY ONE OF THE CITY'S BUSIEST DOWNTOWN INTERSECTIONS HAD THE DISTINCTION OF BEING KNOWN AS THE "FOUR NATIONS" CORNER. THE NAME RESULTED FROM THE FACT THAT THE FOLLOWING STRUCTURES WERE LOCATED AT THIS INTERSECTION; ON THE NORTHWEST CORNER, UPPER CANADA COLLEGE, ON THE SOUTHWEST, GOVERNMENT HOUSE, THE PALATIAL RESIDENCE OF THE PROVINCE'S LIEUTENANT GOVERNOR, ON THE SOUTHEAST, ST. ANDREW'S PRESBYTERIAN CHURCH AND FINALLY ON THE NORTHEAST, THE BRITISH HOTEL AND TAVERN. EDUCATION, LEGISLATION, SALVATION AND...DAMNATION. TODAY, ONLY "SALVATION" SURVIVES.

St. Andrew's Presbyterian Church, southeast corner, c1880.

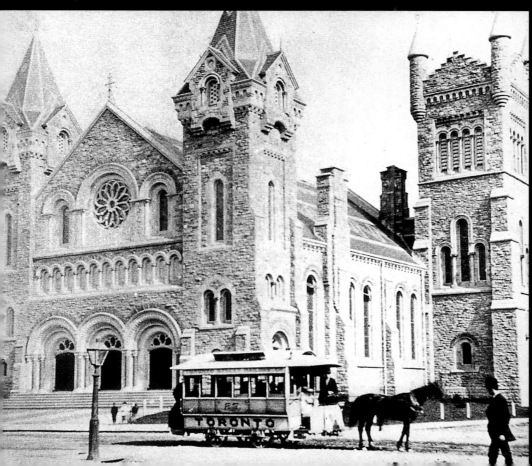

In this photograph, the former Bank of Upper Canada is now home to De La Salle Institute School. Several of the teaching brothers can be seen standing on the porch. The classroom addition to the right of the view was completed the same year this photograph was taken, 1872.

A computer company now occupies the building on the left and the old post office to the right of the photo is once again a post office.

BANK OF UPPER CANADA BUILDING

THERE IS NO DOUBT THAT THE CITY'S MOST HISTORICALLY IMPORTANT ROW OF BUILDINGS CONTINUES TO EXIST ONLY BECAUSE OF THE CONCERN AND ENTHUSIASM SHOWN BY A COUPLE OF TORONTO HISTORY "BUFFS", SHELDON AND JUDY GODFREY. LOCATED AT THE NORTHEAST CORNER OF ADELAIDE AND GEORGE STREETS, THE ROW FEATURES THE BANK OF UPPER CANADA BUILDING WHICH WAS ERECTED IN 1825, THE 1872 DE LA SALLE SCHOOL ADDITION AND THE TOWN OF YORK'S FOURTH POST OFFICE WHICH OPENED FOR BUSINESS ON THIS SITE IN 1833.

In this c.1869 photograph, the Town of York's Fourth Post Office is being used as a residence. Under a magnifying glass, the gentleman on the steps appears to be the occupant of the building, Thomas Denne Harris.

TORONTO'S FIRST POST OFFICE

ONE YEAR LATER (1834), THE TOWN'S ELEVATION TO CITY STATUS RESULTED IN THE BUILDING BECOMING THE HOME OF THE NEW CITY OF TORONTO'S FIRST POST OFFICE. OVER THE FOLLOWING DECADES, THE VARIOUS BUILDINGS IN THIS ROW SERVED AN ASSORTMENT OF USES INCLUDING THOSE DEVOTED TO FINANCIAL, EDUCATIONAL, COMMERCIAL AND AGRICULTURAL PURPOSES. WHEN THE ROW WAS PURCHASED BY SHELDON AND JUDY GODFREY, THE BUILDINGS, ONE OF WHICH HAD BEEN SERIOUSLY DAMAGED BY FIRE IN 1978, WERE ON THE VERGE OF BEING CONDEMNED BY CITY INSPECTORS. THANKS TO THE GODFREYS, THE NECESSARY AND COSTLY REMEDIAL AND RESTORATION WORK QUICKLY GOT UNDERWAY. THE ENTIRE PROJECT TOOK NEARLY 18 MONTHS TO COMPLETE AND SOON THEREAFTER THE BUILDINGS WERE BACK IN BUSINESS. OF PARTICULAR INTEREST IS THE FACT THAT THE OLD POST OFFICE NOW OPERATES AS A PERIOD-STYLE POST OFFICE REMINISCENT OF THE WAY THE MAIL WAS HANDLED BACK IN TORONTO'S EARLIEST DAYS. TOURS ARE GIVEN AND A GIFT SHOP OFFERS PHILATELIC SUPPLIES FOR COLLECTORS AS WELL AS ADDRESSING THE NEEDS OF MODERN-DAY BUSINESSES.

The Fourth Post Office was lovingly restored by the Godfreys and subsequently returned to its role as a "period" post office in 1984, the city's 150th Anniversary Year.

THE GRANGE

Tongues were wagging in the Town of York in 1818 when word got out that D'Arcy Boulton Jr., the eldest son of one of Upper Canada's (Ontario's) most respected jurists, was going to build his new residence (a place he'd call The Grange after a family home in England) on a portion of his 100 acre estate well to the northwest of the townsite. Actually, it wasn't so much what Boulton was going to build, but rather where he was going to build it. Some idea of just how remote the property was can be gained from the fact that the purchase price of the 100 acres (land bounded by the modern Queen Street on the south and Bloor Street on the north, with McCaul and Beverley streets [extended] the east and west boundaries, respectively) was a mere 350 pounds or something less than $2000. Following the death of D'Arcy and his heirs, the old residence in 1911 became the first home of the Art Museum of Toronto (founded in 1900) which has since gone through two name changes and is now the Art Gallery of Ontario. The Grange has been restored to the 1835-40 period and is open to the public.

A formal gathering at the Grange, c1880.

The fully restored Grange as it appears today.

One of the early uses of the old Campbell House was as an office for the Fensom Elevator Works. The company, which later became Otis-Fensom, moved to this location, then 38 Duke Street, in the early 1880s. At other times the house was used as a vinegar warehouse, then as a place to store glass and later still as a horse-nail manufacturing factory.

Campbell House, in its new setting, is open at specific times for public tours. Otherwise it is used by the Advocates' Society for society purposes.

On Easter weekend, 1972, the "ancient" landmark was moved from its original site to its new home on the lawn of the Canada Life building at the northwest corner of Queen Street West and University Avenue. Photo: Larry Milberry

CAMPBELL HOUSE

One of the oldest structures still standing in Toronto (though not on its original site), Campbell House was built in 1822 in what was still called the Town of York for a member of the small town's legal community, William Campbell. As a young man he joined the British military and fought in the American Revolutionary War. After the war, Campbell emigrated to what was then called British North America, pursued a legal and business career and eventually moved to York where he served as a judge for many years. Following his death, the old house was used for a variety of purposes. When plans for the redevelopment of the site were announced in the early 1970s, the lax preservation laws in Ontario, which still exist, meant that the house would either have to be moved to a new site or demolished. Ultimately, thanks to a group of lawyers known as the Advocates' Society, the 300-ton structure was moved more than a mile through the streets of downtown Toronto to a new location that had been set aside for it by the Canada Life Assurance Company. At that time, it was the longest journey by a building of this size in history. Several years later, after an incredible amount of restoration work, the old house, furnished in a style that would have been familiar to Sir William, re-opened to the public.

CASA LOMA

Perched high on the escarpment that once formed the shoreline of prehistoric Lake Iroquois sits Toronto's own romantic castle of stately towers, soaring battlements, secret passageways and sweeping terraces. Casa Loma, "House on the Hill" in Spanish, is a fitting tribute to the dreams, abilities and optimism of the people who built the city – and in particular of Sir Henry Pellatt, who fulfilled a boyhood fantasy by creating a castle between 1911 and 1914 to show he had made it in the nation's business community.

To get ideas for his new home, Sir Henry had toured England, Scotland and France with famed Toronto-born architect Edward James Lennox, paying particular attention to the castles that seemed to appear at every turn in the road. Throughout the trip, Lennox patiently scribbled down his client's architectural likes and dislikes. From this melange, he created Casa Loma, a magnificent, elaborate and truly unique edifice which surpassed any other private home in existence in North America. One critic, however, was to dub the castle a mixture of 17th century Scotland and 20th Century Fox.

With 98 rooms, 30 bathrooms, 25 fireplaces, three bowling alleys, and ovens so big they could cook an entire ox, Sir Henry's mediaeval-style castle was also state-of-the-art. It was wired for electric power, fitted for a central vacuuming system and boasted an elevator and a telephone exchange with 59 telephones – indeed, more phone calls were said to be made in one day at Casa Loma than in the entire rest of the city. Such modern innovation was hardly surprising, given that it was Sir Henry who helped finance the first Canadian generating station at Niagara Falls.

It took three years, three-and-a-half million dollars, and more than 300 workers – each one of whom was personally interviewed by Sir Henry – to build Casa Loma. And it took

More than 400,000 visitors a year experience the magic of 'The Castle', which has been operated as a tourist attraction for more than 60 years by the Kiwanis Club of Casa Loma.

Construction crew posing for a photograph during construction of Casa Loma in the late summer of 1911.

Casa Loma during its very brief - four month - iteration as a hotel in 1929.

Aerial view of Casa Loma's south facade and gardens today.

Winter view of the entrance to Casa Loma c. 1915

less than one decade for him to lose it all – the silver-plated perfume-exuding faucets, the Elizabethan, Chippendale and Louis XIV furniture, and the six hectares (15 acres) of gardens complete with deer, sculptures and fountains. All lost to the economic slump which followed the WW 1. Lost to a reluctant new owner, the city, which actively considered demolishing the structure and selling the land for unpaid property taxes. Lost forever to Sir Henry – but his misfortune was to be the community's gain.

First there was talk of levelling the site for development, then came an offer that would save the building and generate income as well. On August 1, 1929, the castle's massive front doors swung open to welcome guests to the Casa Loma Hotel, whose special attraction was a weekly $2.00 dinner dance featuring canapes, Fresh Lobster Grenoblaise, salad and dessert while Gilbert Watson and His Orchestra played "gay melodies to which nimble feet dance over lovely floors." Unfortunately, however, the reborn castle was blind-sided by the Great Depression and on December 4, just four months after they opened, the castle doors slammed shut once again.

For eight years, "Pellatt's Folly" lay derelict. Then a resourceful Kiwanis Club, on the lookout for a new venture to support local charities, received permission from the city to try to operate the site as a tourist attraction. Their "experiment" became a resounding success and has been ongoing for more than six decades. Today, the restored castle bustles with life, welcoming 400,000 visitors a year, returning approximately one million dollars annually to city coffers and charitable works, and providing a lush setting for movies and marriage ceremonies. During the WW 2, it was also the setting – clandestine, of course – for the manufacturing of a new pre-sonar submarine detection device that helped the Allies win the Battle of the Atlantic. As the engineer who chose the location put it, "Who would suspect a freak castle with dances every Saturday night?"

And what of Sir Henry, who started it all? When he died in 1939, he was living with his former chauffeur in a small suburban house, his assets totalling, some say, $185. However, in a fitting salute to his remarkable abilities and vision, the renowned athlete, acclaimed military leader, adventurous financier and romantic dreamer was accorded the largest funeral Toronto had ever seen.

NEIGHBOURHOODS

One of the things that I really like about Toronto is that it still has a liveable downtown. What I really love to do is just walk along the streets. There is a lot of architectural interest here. I believe that buildings are fossils of human events and reflect the significance of every city.

Author Margaret Atwood

Toronto is blessed by the presence of dozens and dozens of thriving, friendly and exciting neighbourhoods. Some, like Yorkville and Seaton Village, are very old. Cabbagetown, the Beaches and Rosedale are not quite so old and now make up part of the inner city. Others, such as Winston Park, Don Mills and Rexdale, way out in what used to be referred to as the 'burbs, are relatively new. Even newer are the neighbourhoods of Bridletown, West Humber Estates and Rouge River. With the amalgamation of the city and its suburban off-spring in 1998, Toronto became one extended entity. Neighbourhood awareness remains strong however, with street signs and real estate listings helping to perpetuate their existence.

CABBAGETOWN

Once a working-class enclave, Cabbagetown is now a gracious neighbourhood of renovated Victorian homes and lovely parks. It's said that the name came from the cabbages grown on the lawns and in the backyards of the hard working Irish immigrants who, in the 1860-80s, had settled in the present Queen Street East and Don River district. Over time, the community grew in a northwesterly direction as industrialzation moved in.

QUEEN STREET WEST

Queen West is one the city's more popular shopping districts. It features trendy restaurants, cutting-edge fashion, galleries, antique shops and dance clubs. One of the landmarks is the City-TV building, a television studio with many events that spill out onto the street.

House in Cabbagetown
Clarence Roy Greenaway (1891-1972)
Oil on canvas mounted on board, 31.7 x 25.1 cm.
City of Toronto Art Collection

Queen Street West, near Spadina Avenue, Clarence Roy Greenaway (1891-1972). Oil on canvas board, 30.5 x 40.7 cm. City of Toronto Art Collection

Queen Street West
Allen Rutherford Wilbur (1869-1949)
Oil on canvas mounted on board, 28.4 x 20.7 cm.
City of Toronto Art Collection

Ubiquitous streetcar cruising silently past colourful storefronts typical of those found in Queen West Village.

Visitors and locals alike enjoy a pint under a beautiful Saturday afternoon sky on the terrace of the Black Bull.

In 1925 having a pint would have been more a working man's activity carried out in a tavern such as this. Terraces and patios were only to be found in Europe.

Tavern
Clarence Roy Greenaway (1891-1972)
Oil on canvas board, 30.5 x 40.7 cm.
City of Toronto Art Collection

The Black Bull Tavern was built around the same time that York became Toronto, that is 1834. Originally it was located on the city"s outskirts, but as expansion occurred, so too did the number of customers. To accommodate their thirst and the need for a place to stay, the Black Bull was enlarged in 1885 with more alterations sometime around 1910.

Chinatown's neon signs evoke images of Hong Kong.

CHINATOWN

THIS EVER-EXPANDING AREA IS HOME TO ETHNIC CHINESE FROM HONG KONG, SINGAPORE, TAIWAN, VIETNAM AND ELSEWHERE. WITH A WEALTH OF ORIENTAL SHOPS AND OUTDOOR FRUIT MARKETS, IT HAS BECOME ONE OF THE MOST COLOURFUL AND EXCITING PARTS OF THE MODERN CITY. CHINATOWN IS ALSO WELL KNOWN FOR ITS VAST SELECTION OF AUTHENTIC CHINESE RESTAURANTS. TORONTO'S SECOND CHINATOWN IS LOCATED IN THE BROADVIEW/GERRARD AREA AND THREE OTHER DISTINCT CHINATOWNS ARE LOCATED IN THE SUBURBS.

Back in 1878, there was but one person of Chinese descent in the entire City of Toronto. His name was Sam Ching and he operated a hand laundry business in a small shop not far from the busy Bay-Dundas intersection. In the intervening century-and-a-quarter the number of citizens of Chinese descent living in the modern-day Toronto is approaching 200,000. That number now places Toronto ahead of San Francisco as having the largest Chinese community on the continent.

Saturday morning activity on busy Spadina Avenue.

"I'd probably be famous now if I wasn't such a great waitress."

Jane Siberry 1988
Line from the composer and singer's song that recalls her work as a waitress in Toronto before her performing career blossomed.

A TTC streetcar glides down Spadina Avenue having just navigated its way through a crowded Chinatown and across the busy Queen Street West intersection.

In the early 1970s, when the city and the Toronto Transit Commission finally concluded an agreement that would see the streetcar returned to Spadina Avenue, part of the agreement called for the inclusion of 22 pieces of specially commissioned public art to be located at various sites along the street. Each work had to be evocative of the history of the area in which it was placed. In their work titled "Home Again, Home Again", artists David Hlynsky and Shirley Yanover paid tribute to the cat, many of which continue to rule supreme in nearby Kensington Market.

On the far corner in this 1925 view of the Queen and Spadina instersection is the little Mary Pickford movie house, so-named in honour of "America's Sweetheart" who was born right here in Toronto. Before the old building was demolished years later, it served for a time as a discount store called "Bargain Benny's", an "Honest Ed" wanna-be.

KENSINGTON MARKET

The original market dates back to British settlement in the 1890s, when it was a working class district populated primarily by Scottish and Irish labourers which accounts for the very "old country" sounding local street names such as Oxford, Wales, St. Andrews and, of course, Kensington itself. With the end of the WW 1 in sight, the area began to go through another change, this time to satiate the requirements of the workers in the garment district that had developed in the King and Spadina district to the south. Vending stalls were erected in front of the houses where goods and foods of all kinds were offered for sale. People began referring to the area as the "Jewish Market" and so it remained until a new wave of immigrants, this time Portuguese, began arriving in the 1950s. They were followed in the 1960s by newcomers from a variety of Caribbean countries and next by refugees from the carnage in Vietnam. Today the area represents the true meaning of the word eclectic, with people from more than 30 cultural backgrounds, including Portugese, East Indian, African, and Caribbean.

Small shops featuring informal displays of food products reflecting the vast ethnic diversity of the neighbourhood.

Views of High Park's manicured Maple Leaf garden and Grenadier Pond in summer and Fall.

PARKS

A WHOPPING **17** PER CENT OF TORONTO'S URBAN AREA IS GREEN SPACE — THAT'S ALMOST ONE ACRE IN EVERY FIVE, COMPARING EXCEEDINGLY FAVOURABLY WITH THE NORTH AMERICAN AVERAGE OF JUST ONE ACRE IN EVERY **20**. TWO MILLION PEOPLE LIVING IN A FOREST, INDEED.

These "lungs of the city" include some thirteen hundred parks covering more than 7000 hectares (20,000 acres) and ranging in size from the small neighbourhood common to the sprawling ±235 hectare (±575 acre) Toronto Island Park. Among the most innovative, perhaps, is the magical Music Garden which was inspired by world famous cellist Yo Yo Ma. The Garden's layout is a horticultural interpretation of Johann Sebastian Bach's First Suite for Unaccompanied Cello, with each section of the waterfront park inspired by a different movement in the suite. And then there's the Cloud Conservatory, a vast greenhouse oasis in the heart of the downtown core where plants from south Asia and central and south America thrive and inspire in a dreamy, misty milieu.

HIGH PARK

ONE OF TORONTO'S LARGEST PARKS, HIGH PARK REMAINS THE SUBJECT OF A MYTH THAT SEEMS TO GO ON FOREVER. MANY BELIEVE THAT THIS MARVELOUS PIECE OF UNIQUE AND IRREPLACEABLE GREEN SPACE WAS GIVEN TO THE PEOPLE OF THE CITY AS A MAGNANIMOUS GIFT. TO BE HISTORICALLY ACCURATE HOWEVER, JOHN GEORGE HOWARD WASN'T QUITE THAT VIRTUOUS. HOWARD WAS AN ACCOMPLISHED ARCHITECT AND TORONTO'S FIRST SURVEYOR AND ENGINEER, BRINGING BEAUTIFUL BUILDINGS, WOODEN SIDEWALKS AND, EVENTUALLY, PAVED ROADS AND A SEWER SYSTEM TO THE YOUNG CITY. IN 1836, HE PURCHASED FOR HIMSELF A LONG NARROW LOT OF 66.75 HECTARES (165 ACRES) OF PRISTINE FOREST, RAVINES AND SAVANNAH STRETCHING NORTH FROM LAKE ONTARIO BEYOND THE WESTERN EDGE OF THE CITY. THERE HE BUILT HIS HOME, A BEAUTIFUL REGENCY-STYLE "COTTAGE," AND LAID OUT SOME 14 HECTARES (35 ACRES) OF GARDENS. WISELY, HE ENSURED THE SURVIVAL OF HIS WHOLE ESTATE BY BEQUEATHING IT IN 1873 TO THE CITY, "FOR THE FREE USE AND BENEFIT OF THE CITIZENS OF TORONTO FOR EVER." HOWEVER, THE "FREE" PART WOULD ONLY KICK IN FOLLOWING HIS DEATH, WHICH DID NOT OCCUR UNTIL 17 YEARS LATER, BY WHICH TIME HE HAD RECEIVED A TOTAL OF $16,815 IN ANNUAL "PENSION" PAYMENTS FROM THE CITY – A FAR FROM PALTRY SUM IN THOSE DAYS.

In spite of that, there is no doubt that the citizens of Toronto are far and away the biggest winners. High Park, which today embodies almost two-and-a-half times the acreage of the original Howard estate, shelters one of Ontario's last remaining oak savannah habitats and four endangered plant species that are found in only four other places in Canada. Its woodlands and wetlands are a haven for wildlife, its natural beauty a solace for stressed-out urban dwellers, and its manmade features – including a swimming pool, ice rink, tennis courts, outdoor theater, greenhouses and a zoo – are a source of endless interest and diversion. The High Park Adventure Playground is the latest addition, created by children and developed by 3000 volunteers who have celebrated the park's natural environment, history and architecture through the inclusion of original works of art.

Then there's Colborne Lodge, the park's richly-appointed Howard homestead, which boasts among its treasures Toronto's first state-of-the-art bathroom, added in 1854. That same facility now has the distinction of being Toronto's oldest bathroom. And on the grounds of the lodge is the peaceful graveyard which contains John and Jemima Howard's last remains in a sanctuary that is forever closed to the public, at Mr. Howard's request. The site is protected by a fence which once enclosed London's St. Paul's Cathedral in Mr. Howard's native England. That fence not only survived a shipwreck in the St. Lawrence River on its way to the Howard estate, it also is now believed to be the oldest cast iron fence in existence anywhere in the entire world.

For two all-too-brief weeks in October visitors to High Park can look forward to a spectacular display of red and gold.

Throughout the warmer months, wedding parties flock to Edwards Gardens and this magnificent fountain to have their pictures taken. And every bride makes a not so secret plea to the weather gods for the lovely light these people were lucky enough to enjoy.

EDWARDS GARDENS

AMONG THE "YOUNGEST" OF TORONTO'S MAJOR PARKS, THE BEAUTIFUL EDWARDS GARDENS HAS ALREADY MADE A NAME FOR ITSELF AS ONE OF THE FINEST GARDENING EDUCATION CENTERS IN ALL OF CANADA, WITH MORE THAN 14 HECTARES (35 ACRES) OF HANDS-ON GARDENS, A LIBRARY OF SOME 8000 BOTANICAL BOOKS AND PUBLICATIONS, AND MASTER HORTICULTURISTS AT THE READY TO HELP AND ADVISE. THERE'S EVEN A SECTION OF GARDEN ESPECIALLY FOR CHILDREN AND YOUTH, WITH PROJECTS DESIGNED SPECIFICALLY TO MEET SCHOOL SCIENCE CURRICULA. RUPERT E. EDWARDS WOULD BE PARTICULARLY PLEASED BY THE DIRECTION HIS BEAUTIFUL ESTATE HAS TAKEN.

The Canada Varnish Company (remembered in the Leaside street name "Canvarco") had made Edwards a wealthy man and, in 1944, he purchased four-and-a-half hectares (11 acres) of badly overgrown and sadly neglected land in the borough of North York as

Weddings give young girls the chance to be princesses for a day.

Young flower-girl searching for her reflection in one of the garden's lovely fountains.

his country escape. Over the next dozen or so years, he redeemed the property by adding quiet pools, meandering streams, elegant waterfalls, a working waterwheel, wooden arched bridges and – the pièce de résistance – a spectacular 500-foot-long (152-metre) rockery, one of the largest in the country, built over three summers from some 400 tonnes of Credit Valley limestone. An avid golfer, Edwards also laid out a nine hole, par three golf course, portions of which are still visible.

Large sums of money were offered by developers eager to turn the picturesque property into a residential community. One by one, they were turned down. Edwards decided instead to ensure that all weary citizens could take advantage of the restorative power of the landscape he had created and in 1955, he sold the property as a park to the Municipality of Metropolitan Toronto. He received a mere $153,000 for his lands, considerably below the true market value of the day.

JAMES GARDENS

IT WAS A TORONTO FISHMONGER, NO LESS, WHO SAVED A WILDERNESS PROPERTY ON THE BANKS OF THE HUMBER RIVER FROM CERTAIN DESTRUCTION WHEN, C. 1908, HE PURCHASED THE LAND FROM THE HOME SMITH COMPANY, DEVELOPERS OF STATELY HOMES ALONG THE KINGSWAY AND OF THE OLD MILL RESTAURANT. AUGMENTED BY NEIGHBOURING ACREAGE PREVIOUSLY ACQUIRED FROM HIS PARENTS-IN-LAW, THE WHOLE PACKAGE WAS LOVINGLY TRANSFORMED OVER THE NEXT FORTY YEARS BY FRED T. JAMES AND HIS WIFE AS THEY CREATED A FIVE-HECTARE (12-ACRE) HORTICULTURAL SHOWPLACE.

Spring-fed pools, vibrant flower gardens, rare trees, terraced pathways, gazebos and even a fish market (no surprise, really) enticed a constant stream of visitors to their home, "Red Gables," which was built on the property in 1927 of stone gathered from the Humber River. When the couple died in the early 1950s, their wish that the property be kept open for appreciative visitors to enjoy was honoured by the trustees of the estate. The property was sold as a public park to the Municipality of Metropolitan Toronto in 1955 for the sum of $150,000 and the exquisite James Gardens – minus the fish market – became a public park.

ALLAN GARDENS

NOTHING LESS THAN A ROYAL VISIT COULD ADEQUATELY MARK THE GRAND OPENING OF TORONTO'S VERY FIRST CIVIC PARK AND IT WAS NO ONE LESS THAN THE FIRSTBORN SON OF QUEEN VICTORIA, THE PRINCE OF WALES, WHO "DID THE HONOURS" IN THE FALL OF 1860. THE TORONTO HORTICULTURAL SOCIETY HAD SPENT TWO YEARS FULFILLING THE WISHES OF GEORGE ALLAN, AN AVID HORTICULTURIST AND FORMER MAYOR OF THE CITY, WHO HAD GENEROUSLY OFFERED TWO HECTARES (FIVE ACRES) OF HIS CITY PROPERTY ON CONDITION THAT THE ORGANIZATION DEVELOP THE LAND INTO A GARDEN FOR ALL TO ENJOY. BY 1879, IT SEEMED THE WHOLE CITY WAS DOING JUST THAT. THE HORTICULTURAL GARDENS HAD BECOME THE MOST POPULAR SPOT IN TOWN FOR CONCERTS, DRAMATIC PERFORMANCES, OPERAS, GALA BALLS AND VARIOUS OTHER LARGE SOCIAL GATHERINGS, THANKS IN LARGE MEASURE TO THE PRESENCE IN THE MIDDLE OF THE PROPERTY OF A GRAND HORTICULTURAL PAVILION CONSTRUCTED OF WOOD, IRON AND GLASS IN PROPORTIONS LARGE ENOUGH TO ACCOMMODATE SUCH EVENTS. FOLLOWING ALLAN'S DEATH IN 1901, THE MUCH-ENJOYED PARK WAS RENAMED IN HIS HONOUR.

A little less than a year later, much of this happy activity came to an abrupt end when a disastrous fire destroyed the pavilion. The city, which had taken over responsibility for the park some 14 years earlier, replaced the structure with one perhaps more in tune with Allan's botanical bent – an elegant Victorian Palm House. Since then, the purchase of additional lands has increased the luxuriant downtown park to five-and-a-quarter hectares (13 acres), including more than one-third of an acre under glass. In addition the architecturally- and horticulturally-esteemed, heritage-designated Palm House continues to attract considerable attention – not only for its classical proportions but also for the host of exotic plants it contains, including a prized Queen Sago cycad believed to be hundreds of years old.

View of the front of the original Palm House c.1910.

Wooded Path, High Park, Toronto, 1903
John Wycliffe Lowes Forster (1850-1938)
Oil on canvas laid on board, 34.6 x 24.0 cm.
City of Toronto Art Collection

F.H. Varley, A.Y. Jackson, Lawren Harris, Barker Fairley (not a member of the Group of Seven), Frank Johnston, Arthur Lismer, and J.E.H. MacDonald at the Arts & Letters Club, c. 1920. Photo: Arthur Goss/ Arts & Letters Club, Toronto McMichael Canadian Art Collection Archives.

GROUP OF SEVEN

The original seven members were Carmichael, Harris, Jackson, Johnston, Lismer, MacDonald and Varley. Tom Thomson, whose tragic death in 1917 precluded his membership, was an inspiration to the Group. Later additions were A.J. Casson, Edwin Holgate and LeMoine Fitzgerald. A gallery dedicated to the Group - the McMichael Canadian Collection in Kleinburg, just north of Toronto - is another wonderful addition to the many attractions this city has to offer.

Man enjoying a quiet moment by a fountain in Queen's Park.

Leaside (1924)
Alfred Joseph Casson (1898-1992)
Oil on wood panel, 24.0 x 29.0 cm.
City of Toronto Art Collection

Urban planners the world over have long recognized the value of parks and green spaces to city dwellers and all the great cities of the world reflect this philosophy. For people unable to travel to the wilderness locations imortalized by the Group of Seven and myriad other talented artists who devote themselves to the vast array of canadian landscapes, a park bench will go a long way to bringing the same kind of peace and joy not associated with the pace and noise of city streets.

The Legislative Building of Ontario, 2000.

QUEEN'S PARK

THOUGH A GEOGRAPHICALLY INCORRECT TITLE (QUEEN'S PARK IS ACTUALLY A NEARBY CITY PARK THAT WAS OPENED IN 1860 BY THE PRINCE OF WALES AND NAMED IN HONOUR OF HIS MOTHER, QUEEN VICTORIA), THIS TERM HAS BEEN USED FOR MORE THAN A CENTURY TO DESCRIBE THE LEGISLATIVE BUILDING OF ONTARIO, THE MEETING PLACE FOR ONTARIO'S PARLIAMENT SINCE THE BUILDING'S OFFICIAL OPENING IN 1893. IT WAS DESIGNED BY RICHARD WAITE IN THE ROMANESQUE REVIVAL STYLE AND TOOK SIX YEARS TO CONSTRUCT AT A COST OF APPROXIMATELY $1.3 MILLION, JUST ABOUT HALF THE COST OF TORONTO'S NEW CITY HALL ERECTED JUST SIX YEARS LATER. A SERIOUS FIRE IN 1909 DESTROYED MUCH OF THE WEST WING. TODAY'S LEGISLATIVE BUILDING IS ONE OF MANY LOCATIONS IN WHICH ONTARIO'S PARLIAMENT HAS MET SINCE THE PROVINCE'S CREATION (AS THE PROVINCE OF UPPER CANADA) IN 1791. SOME OF THE TORONTO SITES INCLUDE THE SO-CALLED PALACE OF GOVERNMENT AT THE FOOT OF TODAY'S PARLIAMENT STREET (THUS THE NAME OF THE STREET), JORDAN'S HOTEL (WHERE THE TORONTO SUN BUILDING NOW STANDS ON KING STREET EAST), THE OLD YORK GENERAL HOSPITAL ON KING STREET WEST AND, IN 1832, THE NEWLY ERECTED LEGISLATIVE BUILDINGS ON FRONT STREET JUST WEST OF SIMCOE, AN AREA OF TOWN KNOWN FOR A TIME AS SIMCOE PLACE.

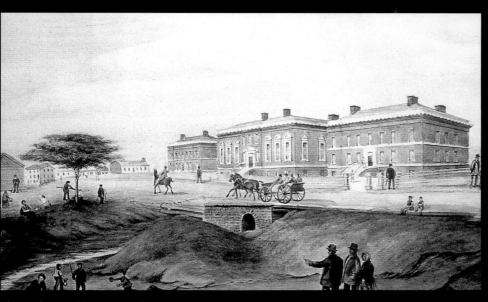

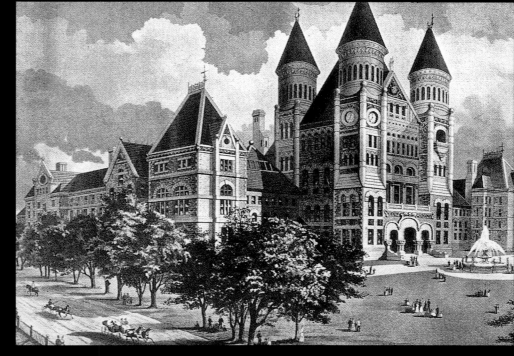

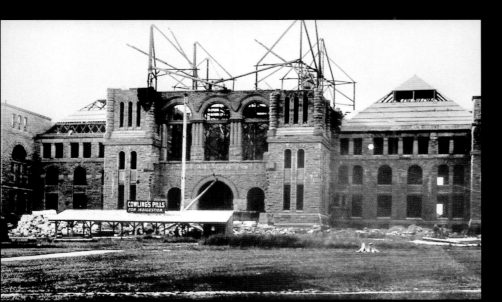

The Legislative Buildings, Simcoe Place, Front Street West, c1832.

Preliminary plans for the new building featured a clock in the west tower and a large fountain near the main entrance. Budget cuts precluded both.

COWLING'S PILLS
FOR INDIGESTION

Aerial view of the Legislative Building of Ontario looking to the north. The multitude of trees at the top of the photograph is Queen's Park. To the right are other Ontario government buildings and to the left, a small portion of the grounds and buildings of the University of Toronto.

Sir John A. Macdonald looking south along University Avenue at all the trees, c1914.

Needless to say, there have been remarkable changes to the University Avenue streetscape since Hamilton MacCarthy's statue of Sir John A. Macdonald was unveiled in 1894, just one year after the Parliament Building opened. In fact, the street itself has changed. In the earlier view, we see what was originally a private thoroughfare connecting Queen Street with the University of King's College (this pioneer Toronto educational facility occupied a building that was located where the Parliament Building stands today and was the forerunner of the present University of Toronto). Over the years, College Avenue, as it was then called, evolved into a route now occupied by the southbound lanes of the modern University Avenue. For many years the municipality provided an endowment to the university for the public's use of this thoroughfare, though the school kept close control over what was built on the adjacent lands. Today's northbound lanes occupy all of what was a narrow public street (visible in the trees to the left of the view) called Park Lane or, at times, University Street. Eventually, all these lovely trees were cut down and the two once separate streets combined into one. The proliferation of hospitals on both sides of the north end of the present University Avenue has resulted in a new nickname for this part of the street, "Bed Pan Alley".

Sir John looking for all the trees, 2000.

Looking north on University Avenue from the new Canada Life Assurance Building, west side north of Queen. 1930. Visible in this photograph are the Legislative Building of Ontario (top of the street), a portion of the Toronto General Hospital (east side, south of College Street) and, in the lower right foreground, the University Avenue synagogue.

Similar view today. An insurance tower blocks out the Parliament Buildings while at the lower right is the University Avenue Court House which was erected on the site of the illustrious University Avenue Armoury in the mid-1960s (a period of time when Toronto lost many of its fine old buildings).

Aerial view of the busy Avenue Road/Bloor Street intersection, c1945.

In the contemporary aerial view, many office and condominium towers have been added to the area.

BLOOR & AVENUE ROAD

The tall building at the northwest corner of the intersection in the 1945 photograph is the Park Plaza Hotel which, though completed in 1929, was plagued by structural problems caused by Taddle Creek, an underground stream that over time has affected several major Toronto structures. Though the problem was solved, the hotel was unable to welcome its first guests until 1936. A recent multi-million dollar renovation and restoration project has transformed the tired old hotel into one of the city's finest and it now, as the Park Hyatt Toronto Hotel, eagerly welcomes a whole new generation of guests.

Across Avenue Road to the east is the charming Church of the Redeemer which opened at what was still just a dusty cross-roads in 1879.

On the southeast corner is the former Lillian Massey School of Household Science completed in 1912 and financed by the daughter of Hart Massey of the Massey Manufacturing Company (and Massey Hall and Fred Victor Mission) fame.

The Royal Ontario Museum (the first two phases of which were completed in 1914 and 1932) occupies the remaining corner.

UNIVERSITY OF TORONTO

An educated ruling class was deemed to be essential by John Strachan, the Scottish-born teacher and clergyman who in 1827, twenty years after the establishment of the city's very first school, obtained a royal charter for the establishment of King's College, Upper Canada's first institution of higher learning and predecessor of the University of Toronto. Just 14 years earlier, this natural born leader, in the absence of any British military presence following the American takeover of York in 1813, had singlehandedly negotiated an end to the burning of the town with the occupying general. By 1827, he was a respected and highly influential presence in the community and would later become the city's first Church of England bishop. However, the money to staff and build his college would not be available for more than another decade.

Meanwhile, the province underwent a very Canadian, relatively peaceful version of a war of independence, markedly different from the bloody conflict our American cousins had experienced some five decades earlier. A consensus was slowly building that the colony could become internally self-governing while remaining part of the British Empire, that it could have locally-grown policies that were at variance with London and could trade with others besides Britain and still be loyal to the Crown, and that it was time for the old world order of power and hierarchy headed by church and aristocracy to come to an end in new world Upper Canada. Strachan's King's College, which finally opened in 1843 and granted its first degrees the following year, came to epitomise the outdated old order, governed as it was by the Anglican Church. And so, with one stroke of the pen, the provincial government converted the college on January 1, 1850 into a nondenominational educational institute complete with a new name, the University of Toronto. Within a year, however, old order follower John Strachan had founded yet another seat of learning, Trinity College, for the Anglican Church.

The passage of a few decades mellowed the strident controversy over secular versus ecclesiastic higher education, several church colleges uniting with the secular University of Toronto completely voluntarily and for acknowledged mutual benefit. The first, in 1892, was Victoria College, founded by the Methodist Church some 50 years earlier. Next came St. Michael's, founded in 1852 by the Roman Catholic Church. These were followed in 1906 by John Strachan's own Trinity College – but fortunately, for his sake, Bishop Strachan was long gone by that time. Others to federate with the university would eventually include the Knox (Presbyterian), Wycliffe (Anglican) and Emmanuel (United Church of Canada) colleges of theology.

Today, having also embraced the independent New, Massey and Innis colleges in the 1960s, the University of Toronto is Canada's largest university and the fifth largest in North America. It has an enrolment of more than 50,000 graduate and undergraduate students in seven colleges spread over three campuses. The main campus is the downtown 50-hectare (123.6-acre) St. George campus with 121 buildings including the beautiful Neo-Gothic Hart House, the students' home away from the classroom – a unique cultural, social and recreational facility initiated by Vincent Massey, who would become Canada's Governor General, and named in memory of his grandfather, Hart Massey, philanthropist and renowned manufacturer of agricultural implements. The other two campuses are at Scarborough, which opened in 1964 some 33 kilometres to the east of downtown, and at Erindale, founded two years later about 33 kilometres to the west.

Aerial views of the University of Toronto's St. George campus today and c.1950 (below). In both views College Street is at the bottom with King's College Road running perpendicular to it, north to the Front Campus. To the left is St. George Street. On the north side of the Front Campus is University College, a Toronto landmark since 1859. At the southwest corner of the campus is Convocation Hall, completed in 1907. Off the campus to the right is the Ontario Legislative Building, site of King's College, the 1829 forerunner of the present U of T. When the university was secularized in 1850, students and teachers abandoned the old King's College building. For a time it was used as an asylum prior to being razed and the Legislative Building erected on the site. (We're still not sure all the inmates left.)

Aerial view of the site of another new City Hall for Toronto in 1961. Note, the 1899 City Hall at top left and the row of pawnshops and old theatres on the south side of Queen Street, an area now occupied by the Sheraton Centre.

Aerial view of New City Hall and Nathan Phillips Square as they appear today.

CITY HALL

HAD HE LIVED TO SEE IT, GEORGE ORWELL WOULD HAVE FELT VINDICATED BY THE DESIGN OF TORONTO'S DISTINCTIVE CITY HALL, OPENED TO INTERNATIONAL ACCLAIM IN 1965. THE DRAMATIC STRUCTURE WAS DESIGNED TO REPRESENT A GIANT EYE — "THE EYE OF GOVERNMENT," NO LESS — WHEN VIEWED FROM THE AIR, ITS EXPANSIVE CIRCULAR COUNCIL CHAMBER NUCLEUS RIMMED BY TWO STRIKINGLY CURVED OFFICE TOWERS. UNANIMOUSLY SELECTED FROM AMONG ARCHITECTURAL SUBMISSIONS RECEIVED FROM 42 COUNTRIES, FINN VILJO REVELL'S VISIONARY (PARDON THE PUN) COMPLEX BUILT ON FIVE HECTARES (12.75 ACRES) OF HEART-OF-THE-CITY LAND IMMEDIATELY BECAME ONE OF TORONTO'S MOST RECOGNIZABLE ARCHITECTURAL ICONS. INDEED, IN 1998, A STYLIZED VERSION OF THE BUILDING WAS ADOPTED OVERWHELMINGLY BY THE COMMUNITY AS THE OFFICIAL LOGO OF THE RECENTLY EXPANDED CITY.

If it's true that "great buildings symbolize a people's deeds and aspirations," as proclaimed at the official opening of the new City Hall, then this celebrated modern complex, viewed from the ground, surely speaks of the creativity, confidence and inclusiveness that have made Toronto the most powerful of Canadian cities. However, when Toronto Mayor John Shaw made this observation, the year was 1899 and he was referring to the new City Hall of that era, a spectacular Romanesque Revival building designed by Edward James Lennox, who later built two other splendid Toronto landmarks, Casa Loma and the King Edward Hotel.

In 1899, Lennox's combined City Hall and Courthouse at the corner of Queen Street and Bay was not only the largest structure in Toronto at the time, it was also the largest municipal building in the whole of North America. With exquisite architectural detailing both inside and out, the castle-like edifice was recognized as one of the most magnificent buildings on the continent.

Similar view soon after City Hall opened for business on September 18, 1899.

Similar view of the Old City Hall 100 years on.

View of Toronto's new City Hall looking northwest from the corner of Queen and James, c1895. Squabbles and bickering would prevent the building from being ready for use for another four years.

Mayor Shaw no doubt appreciated its grandeur as a reflection of turn-of-the-century society's innocent and optimistic confidence in the might of authority, a sentiment clearly shared by other members of a council, one of whom was so overcome by emotion during the opening ceremonies that the mayor had to order his removal.

With the opening of the current City Hall in 1965, however, this grand old building suffered the indignity of being designated "disposable" in order to accommodate the rapidly expanding world of commerce – i.e. to make way for a shopping centre. The Friends of Old City Hall, a group of tenacious volunteers, fought the demolition armed with little more than buckets of soap and water. After they had washed away seven decades' worth of accumulated grime from a section of the facade, the true stature of Lennox's creation was once again visible, public sentiment in the building's favour grew, and before long its future was assured. In 1989, its timeless beauty and historic significance were protected for posterity when it was officially designated a National Historic Site and it continues to serve the community as a courthouse to this day.

NATHAN PHILIPS SQUARE

The idea of a new city hall for Toronto was an old idea and the concept of a civic square was even older. And while the electorate sanctioned building the square as early as 1947, it wasn't until the elections of 1957 that the voters, who had rejected the new city hall idea in 1956, were finally convinced to give the idea the go ahead. The force behind this approval was a long-time city politician, Nathan Phillips, who was first elected to city council back in 1924. In 1955, he was elected mayor and immediately began looking at ways to have a new city hall built. Through his efforts, the new city hall project was approved by a majority of over 5,000 votes. In short order an international competition was announced, another Phillips' idea and one that brought howls of disapproval from many Canadian architects. Nevertheless, a total of 532 applicants responded to the competition notice and from all the designs submitted eight finalists were selected. From those, a jury of five eminent architects selected the unusual, yet innovative concept presented by Finnish architect Viljo Revell. Revell's plan also included a public square in front of city hall. To honour the man who had laid it all on the line in his ongoing crusade to get Toronto its new city hall, council members unanimously agreed to name the 4.65 hectare (11 acre) public space 'Nathan Phillips Square'.

The reflecting pool on Nathan Phillips Square becomes a skating rink in the winter.

The 91.4 meter (300 foot) high clock tower of Old City Hall looks down on summertime visitors to Nathan Phillips Square.

Nathan Phillips Square from the air.

Looking east from atop the Canada Life Assurance Building on University Avenue towards City Hall, c.1929. One of the buildings demolished to make way for Toronto's new City Hall was the Registry Office, the handsome structure seen to the left of this photograph. It was completed in 1917 and was to be the first structure in a proposed civic government complex of palatial buildings that were to be constructed at the apex of a new street, Federal Avenue, that would run north from the new Union Station. The street never materialized, nor did any of the civic buildings except for the Registry Office. It remained an orphan for more than 4 decades until demolished to make way for a civic building, the city's new City Hall.

Topping off the Canada Life Assurance Building on University Avenue in 1929. Note the absence of hard hats and safety equipment.

Aerial view looking east to New City Hall and Nathan Phillips Square today. Canada Life Assurance Building on University Avenue (vantage point for the photo above and on the opposite page) is visible at the bottom right of this photo.

Looking east from atop the Canada Life Assurance Building today. The Registry office has vanished to be replaced by the northwest corner of Nathan Phillips Square. The Sheraton Centre is to the right on Queen Street. Note that Old City Hall appears in both photographs.

THE CENOTAPH

For the first few years following the end of the Great War, city officials erected a temporary memorial to Toronto's war dead around which grieving citizens would place wreaths and other symbols of remembrance. The idea of a permanent structure was first proposed by Alderman George Shields and approved by city council in the summer of 1924 at a cost not to exceed $25,000. The Ontario Association of Architects administered the competition for the most fitting design for the city's new Soldiers' Memorial Cenotaph (the official name with the term cenotaph derived from the Greek for "empty tomb"). A total of 20 designs was submitted, the winner being that of the local architectural firm of Ferguson and Pomphrey. Designed after the style of the Great Cenotaph in London, England and sculpted from Canadian Shield granite by Toronto's McIntosh Granite Company, the cornerstone of the memorial was tapped into place on June 24, 1925 by Field Marshall the Earl Haig, Commander-in-Chief of the British Forces in the Great War. The following Remembrance Day, Toronto's new Cenotaph (which, incidentally, came in nearly $8,000 under budget, one of the few civic projects in history able to make that claim) was dedicated with great ceremony by Lord Byng, then Governor General of Canada. Originally inscribed with a few simple words "To Our Glorious Dead" and several engagements in which Torontonians played a valiant part, the Cenotaph now also features references to the WW 2 and the Korean War.

Torontonians gather in front of City Hall to watch as the Earl Haig places the cornerstone for the city's new war memorial. June 25, 1925.

Though there have been several attempts to relocate Toronto's Cenotaph it still maintains its place of prominence in front of Old City Hall.

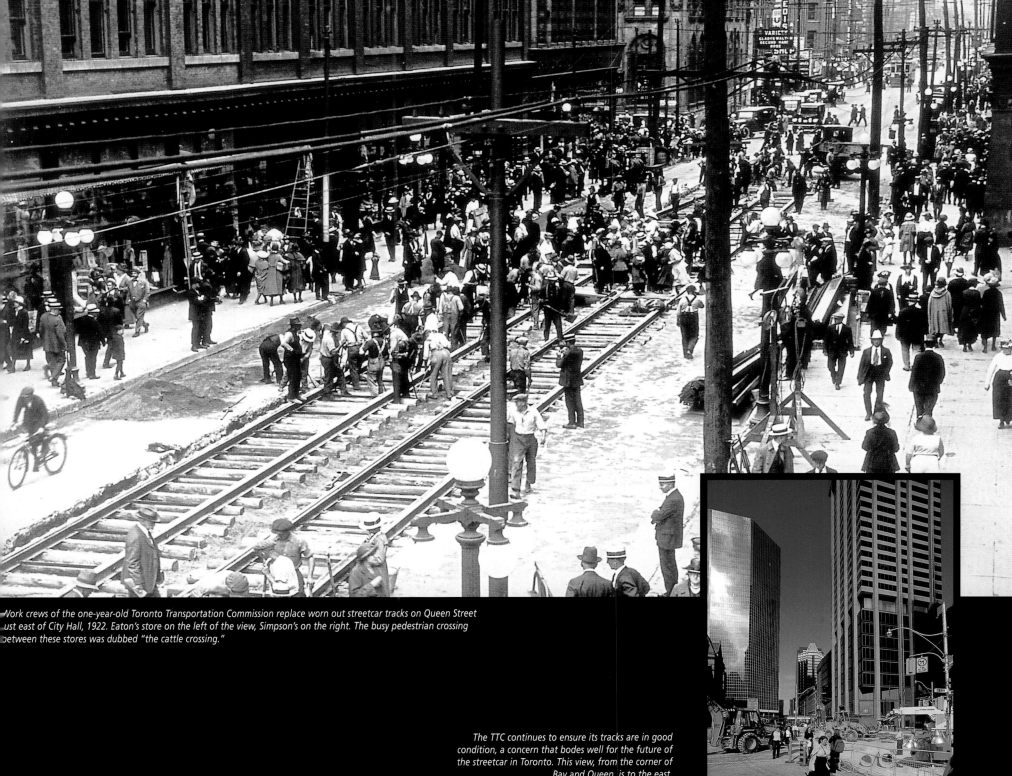

Work crews of the one-year-old Toronto Transportation Commission replace worn out streetcar tracks on Queen Street just east of City Hall, 1922. Eaton's store on the left of the view, Simpson's on the right. The busy pedestrian crossing between these stores was dubbed "the cattle crossing."

The TTC continues to ensure its tracks are in good condition, a concern that bodes well for the future of the streetcar in Toronto. This view, from the corner of Bay and Queen, is to the east.

The oldest surviving City Hall is located at the southwest corner of Front Street and Jarvis and still serves a community purpose. Constructed in 1845 to house a young Toronto's municipal offices, with a two-storey-high council chamber on the second floor and a police station on the first, the edifice is now renowned as the city's premier fresh foods outlet, the historic South St. Lawrence Market. Knee-high flooding in the basement prisoners' cells not long after the building opened was the reason for the first of several renovations to the original edifice, which lost its municipal tenants in 1899. It eventually was rebuilt almost beyond recognition to accommodate the growing city's need for a much larger public market. Perhaps the most appropriate renovation took place in the 1970s, when the second-floor council chamber, after lying empty for three-quarters of a century, re-entered public consciousness as the historic Market Gallery, where the municipality's finest art and archival treasures are on public display.

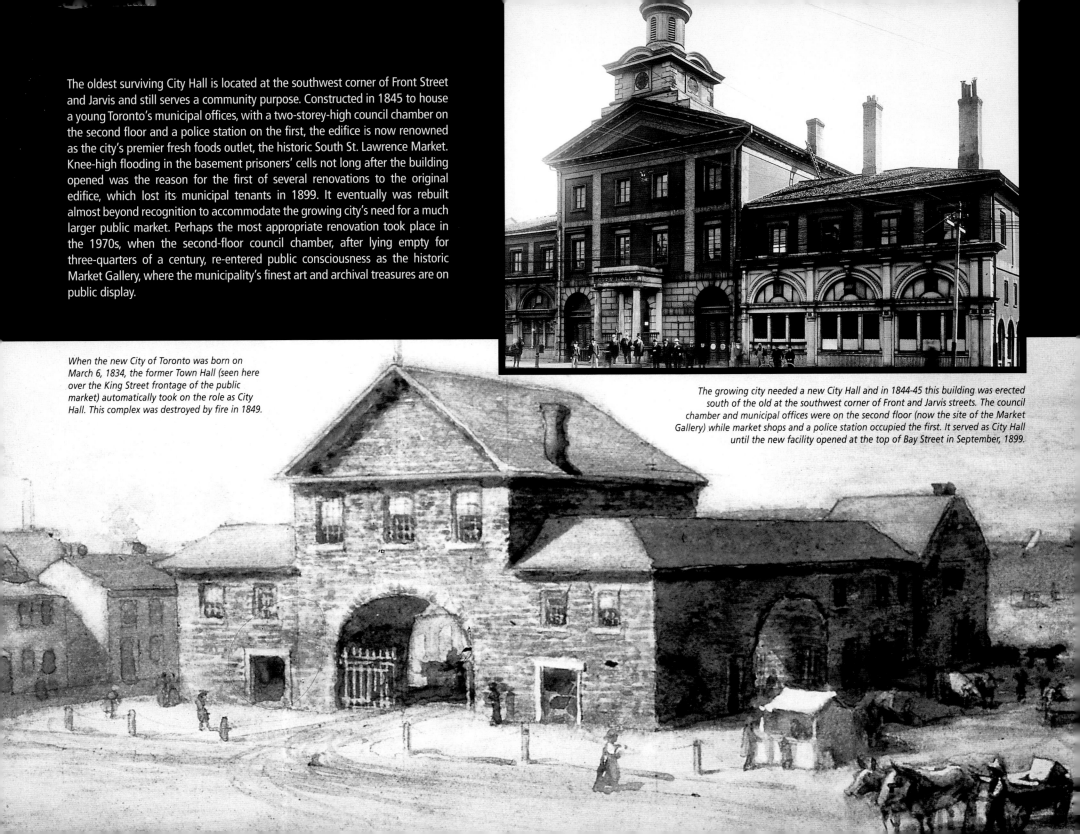

When the new City of Toronto was born on March 6, 1834, the former Town Hall (seen here over the King Street frontage of the public market) automatically took on the role as City Hall. This complex was destroyed by fire in 1849.

The growing city needed a new City Hall and in 1844-45 this building was erected south of the old at the southwest corner of Front and Jarvis streets. The council chamber and municipal offices were on the second floor (now the site of the Market Gallery) while market shops and a police station occupied the first. It served as City Hall until the new facility opened at the top of Bay Street in September, 1899.

Toronto City Hall, Front and Jarvis streets, c1870.

The central portion of the 1844-45 City Hall remains imbedded in the South St. Lawrence Market, c.1965. Photo: Mike Filey.

ST. LAWRENCE MARKET

SATURDAY, NOVEMBER 5, 1803, SAW THE START OF THE UNSHAKEABLE 200-YEARS-AND-COUNTING TORONTO WEEKLY RITUAL OF SHOPPING AT THE LOCAL FARMER'S MARKET. IN FACT, THE MARKET WAS SO IMPORTANT TO THE PEOPLE OF THE CITY THAT THE PROVINCE'S LIEUTENANT GOVERNOR HIMSELF SIGNED A PROCLAMATION THAT SAME YEAR ORDERING A MARKET TO BE HELD EACH AND EVERY SATURDAY ON THE SITE BOUNDED BY FRONT, JARVIS, KING AND CHURCH STREETS, THEREAFTER TO BE KNOWN AS THE MARKET BLOCK. THE SIGNIFICANCE OF THE EXERCISE WAS FURTHER SUBSTANTIATED SOME FIVE DECADES LATER WHEN A NEW MARKET BUILDING WAS CONSTRUCTED AND GIVEN NO LESS A NAME THAN THAT OF CANADA'S MOST SIGNIFICANT SAINT, ITS PATRON SAINT – ST. LAWRENCE.

The first brick market building – the North Market – was erected in 1831 and occupied most of the block. It must have seemed absolutely luxurious to vendors and shoppers alike after three decades under a simple 10.5 metres by six metres (35 feet x 20 feet) wooden shelter which was open to the vagaries of the weather until 1820 when it was enclosed – but even then only on three sides. Indeed, the new brick structure was grand enough and large enough to also house the community's first municipal offices, becoming the first City Hall when the city was incorporated in 1834. However, the edifice was not without its detractors. Some said that the main reason the town was elevated to city status was so

that additional taxes could be levied to help pay for this extravagant structure which had cost taxpayers £9240 (approximately $46,000), a figure that some felt was outrageously high for a community of nine thousand souls. One can only imagine what their emotions would have been had they known it would all be burned to the ground less than 20 years later. By then, however, an even larger City Hall had been constructed across the way, on the south side of Front Street at Jarvis, with market stalls – the South Market – at the rear for the sale of fruits, vegetables and poultry. By then, however, the population had soared to some 25,000.

The burnt-out North Market was replaced in 1850-1851 and included a magnificent cultural centre complete with Corinthian columns, a distinctive cupola and a two-storeys-high Great Hall. It was at this point that the whole complex was given the significant "St. Lawrence" name and the elegant St. Lawrence Hall quickly became the social hub of the young city, hosting concerts, exhibitions, lectures and public meetings. It was here that numerous orators railed against slavery. And it was here that John A. Macdonald, who was to become Canada's first Prime Minister in 1867, promoted the confederation of the provinces.

Looking north to the St. Lawrence Market from Front Street, c1875. Now a pedestrian walkway, this thoroughfare was originally called, for obvious reasons, Market Street.

The St. Lawrence Hall, the city's social centre until relegated to second place in 1893 by the new Massey Hall. Note the canopy over Front Street connecting the North and South St. Lawrence Markets. Installed for the convenience of shoppers during bad weather, it was declared unsafe by city inspectors, the canopy was demolished in 1954.

The restoration of the St. Lawrence Hall, one of the city's 1967 Centennial projects, was almost terminated when, in the spring of 1967, the entire east wall collapsed sending bricks and mortar flying into the afternoon rush hour traffic.

Meanwhile, over at the North Market, as other cultural venues came along and displaced the St. Lawrence Hall in popularity, several decades of neglect befell that landmark building. Then Canada's centennial anniversary approached and people began taking a second look at the structures which had played a role in the making of the nation's history. The City of Toronto, aided and abetted by the Toronto Construction Association and the local chapter of the Ontario Association of Architects, decided that restoring the Hall would be the perfect way to mark the centennial and, after some fits and starts, work got underway in the summer 1966.

The project almost came to a halt late in the afternoon of March 10, 1967, however, when a large portion of the east wall cascaded into the busy King Street and Jarvis intersection, miraculously hurting no one but for a time threatening to make the project itself a victim of the disaster. Fortunately, momentum to restore this venerable landmark was overwhelming and today its compelling architecture, rich fittings, glittering gas-lit crystal chandelier and ornate plaster ceilings impress 21st century visitors just as much as they did those of the 19th century.

The adjoining market building, however, wasn't so lucky. The North Market was demolished in 1900, rebuilt in 1904, demolished in 1968 and then rebuilt yet again. Today, in it's fifth incarnation, it still houses the historic Saturday Farmer's Market, as it has always done throughout the past 200 years. And on Sundays, appropriately enough, it offers history for sale in the form of antiques.

"I had been accustomed to see hundreds of Indians about my native village, then Little York, muddy and dirty, just struggling into existence, now the City of Toronto, bursting forth in all its energy and commercial strength."

Paul Kane
Artist comparing the changes in the community between 1844 and 1859.

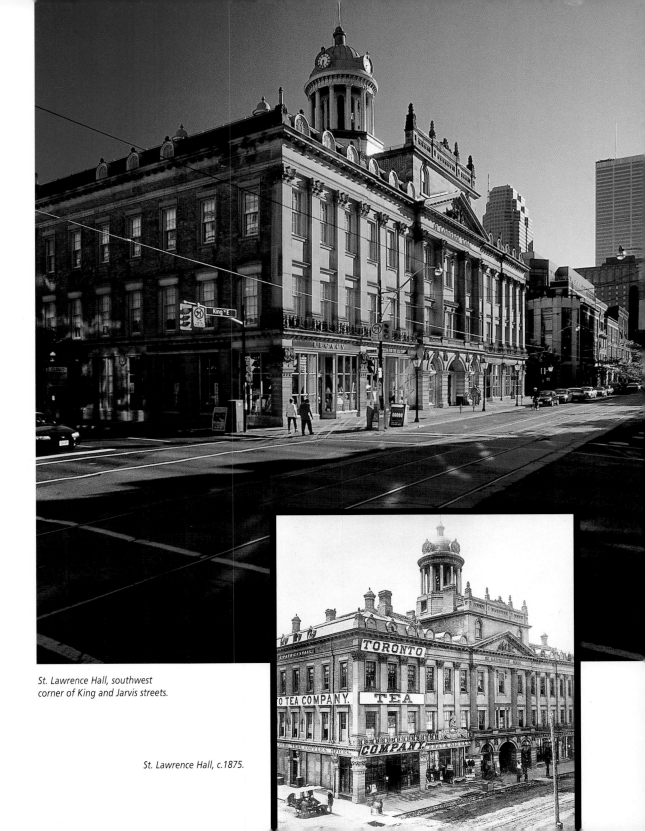

St. Lawrence Hall, southwest corner of King and Jarvis streets.

St. Lawrence Hall, c.1875.

When the City Hall vacated the South Market building for even larger premises in 1899, that venue too really came into its own. Market stalls expanded from the spot they had been assigned at the rear of the building and quickly took over the whole site, which in fact had to be enlarged to accommodate the demands of a growing city's need to feed itself. Over the next 50 years, the South Market never looked back. Then came the advent of competition in the form of supermarkets, followed by a consultant's report which advised demolition over renovation. The writing appeared to be on the wall. That's when Time and Place, a determined group of farsighted history lovers who chose urban revitalization over urban renewal, sprang into being. They persuaded the city to renovate the building – an exercise which included extensive work on almost an acre of roof – and to return the second floor Council Chamber, derelict for 70 years, to its former glory. Today, the South Market is more popular than ever, even the basement's former prisoners' cells are called into action five days a week to meet the demand of discriminating citizens seeking fresh foods imported from around the world as well as local delicacies, arts and crafts.

Close-up of King Street facade of the St. Lawrence Hall today. Note gas lights, the method of street illumination in use when the Hall opened in 1851.

South St. Lawrence Market at the southwest corner of Front and Jarvis streets. The buff-coloured bricks outline the 1844-45 City Hall.

"I've circled the planed Earth forty-four times and I can honestly say that Toronto right now is operating better than any other city in the world. I don't know how long Toronto's golden moment will last. But, for the moment, it's the most comfortable city to live in. It's the cleanest city. And it works."

R. Buckminster Fuller

Interior of the South St. Lawrence Market, 2000.

and 2000. In the distance is City Hall, a portion of which has been incorporated into the South St. Lawrence Market that now stands on its site. Many of the buildings along the south side of Front Street were constructed in the 1860s and 1870s, their rear walls rising from the edge of the old Toronto Bay. Condominium units now fill the 1861 warehouse at 81-83 Front Street East.

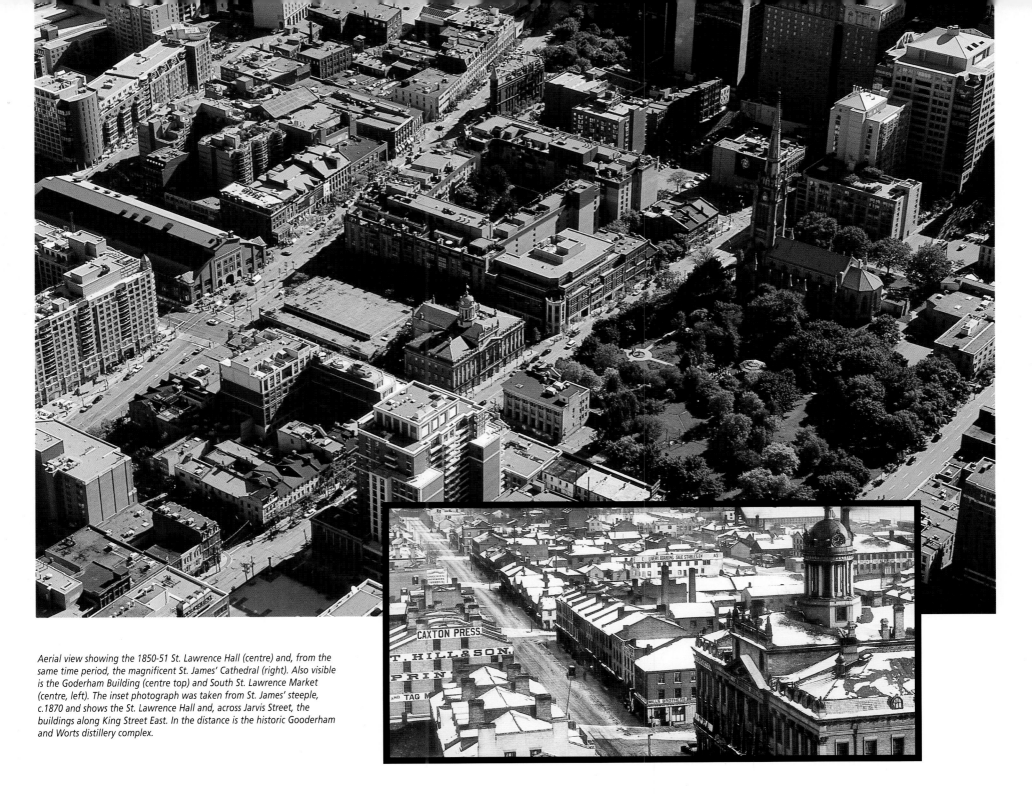

Aerial view showing the 1850-51 St. Lawrence Hall (centre) and, from the same time period, the magnificent St. James' Cathedral (right). Also visible is the Goderham Building (centre top) and South St. Lawrence Market (centre, left). The inset photograph was taken from St. James' steeple, c.1870 and shows the St. Lawrence Hall and, across Jarvis Street, the buildings along King Street East. In the distance is the historic Gooderham and Worts distillery complex.

CAXTON PRESS.

T. HILL & SON.

PRIN

AND TAG M

LIVERY BOARDING SALE STABLES

MILLS BROTHERS

Coffin Block at the corner of Front and Jarvis streets, 1873.

Cooper's Wharf and the Toronto fish market, foot of Church Street, 1838. One of the most frequently seen views of early Toronto is this wonderful painting by William Henry Bartlett, an Englishman who travelled extensively in the early part of the 19th century. His trips were often recorded in books he both wrote and illustrated. The accompanying view is of the city's busy fish market which was located on the waterfront just east of the then foot of Church Street. This work appeared in his "Canadian Scenery" which was published in 1842, a year often used to date all the illustrations in the book. In fact, all the paintings in the book depict places and events as they appeared during his visit to Upper Canada (Ontario), Lower Canada (Quebec) and the Maritimes four years earlier. To the extreme right of the painting reproduced here is the City Hotel (formerly the Steamboat Hotel) which was located on the north side of Front Street just east of Church. To the left of it is a wooden commercial structure that many referred to as the "Coffin Block" because of its unusual shape resulting from the convergence of Front and Wellington streets. This building was the terminal for the Kingston-Toronto stage coach service that arrived in town via, that's right, the Kingston Road.

"Coffin Block". Cross-referencing the business signs on the "Coffin Block" with city directories reveal that this photograph was taken c1890.

Since 1973, Canada's majors banks and their architects have been busy providing a new back drop for the historic Gooderham Building.

Officially titled the Gooderham Building, most Torontonians know this structure better as the "Flatiron Building", a name that describes its unique shape. In this c.1975 view the CN Tower is still under construction in the background. Photo: Larry Milberry

GOODERHAM & WORTS

Painting depicting busy harbour activity around the Gooderham & Worts Distillery in 1896.

THE STORY OF GOODERHAM AND WORTS BEGINS WITH JAMES WORTS EMIGRATING FROM ENGLAND IN 1831 TO YORK (TORONTO), UPPER CANADA. UPON ARRIVAL, HE ACQUIRED LOW-LYING LAND NEAR THE MOUTH OF THE DON RIVER AND SET ABOUT BUILDING A RED BRICK WINDMILL. IT WOULD RISE OVER 20 METRES HIGH AND BECOME A PROMINENT LANDMARK IN THE YOUNG CITY. WORTS WAS JOINED A YEAR LATER BY HIS BROTHER-IN-LAW, WILLIAM GOODERHAM AND TOGETHER THEY SOON BEGAN THEIR DISTILLING BUSINESS BY DIRECTING SURPLUS AND POOR QUALITY GRAIN TO THE MAKING OF WHISKY, GIVING RISE TO WHAT WOULD BECOME A RENOWNED DISTILLING OPERATION

By 1867, as the fledgling Canada was being forged, railways had become the main mode of transport, and Gooderham and Worts was shipping whisky across Ontario, Canada, the U.S. and the Empire.

In 1988, Gooderham and Worts became a national historic site, and the owners, Allied Domecq, shifted their focus to historic preservation, rather than production. Gooderham and Worts, Canada's largest 19th century distilling firm, was closed down permanently in 1990. The old distillery and several other ancillary structures still stand and are being incorporated into a new residential/retail marketplace complex.

Aerial view looking north up Parliament Street in 1929. The distillery can be seen in the foreground area to the east of Parliament.

Similar view today. Parliament Street runs north under the Gardiner Expressway from the v-shaped slip in the foreground. The distillery property is being developed as a multi-use, residential and business complex.

SHOPPING

SHOPPING TODAY IS A SNAP. JUST JUMP INTO THE CAR AND HEAD OFF TO THE NEAREST CORNER STORE. NEED SOMETHING SPECIAL? DRIVE A LITTLE FURTHER AND YOU'RE SURE TO FIND IT IN ONE OF THE NUMEROUS SHOPPING CENTRES OR REGIONAL MALLS IN AND AROUND THE CITY. IN A FEW YEARS, MOST PEOPLE WON'T EVEN HAVE TO LEAVE THE HOUSE TO SHOP. THEY'LL SIMPLY BOOT UP THE COMPUTER AND DO THEIR SHOPPING ON-LINE. NO DOUBT THIS'LL BE A FAR BETTER WAY TO SHOP THAN THE WAY IT WAS DONE IN THE OLDEN DAYS. OR WILL IT BE?

Artist J. D. Kelly's representation of the French trading with the aboriginal people at Fort Rouillé (also known as Fort Toronto), a small pallisaded structure that stood near the site of the present CNE Bandshell from 1750 until destroyed by the French in 1759.

The delivery wagons of the Robert Simpson Company, each of which was drawn by a magnificent dapple grey horse, line up along Richmond Street where parcels were loaded for the day's deliveries, c1905.

Eaton's delivery wagons, on the other hand, were pulled by chestnuts, a few of which are still active in this 1913 photograph taken at the corner of Albert and James streets, behind the main store. The conversion to gasoline-powered vehicles has obviously started, which is probably more than can be said for some of the trucks, one of which uses a horse blanket as an engine warmer.

For instance, when you wanted milk or butter, bread or ice back then you simply placed a sign in the window that tersely stated MILK, or when turned upside down, NO MILK. It was the same procedure for butter and ice. Every now and then, just like clockwork, the milkman, breadman or iceman, doing the rounds with his wagon full of products and drawn by a horse that was almost as clever as the driver, would spot the sign and do your bidding. Even fresh produce came to the house via a horse-drawn wagon. It was just as easy to order on line from Eaton's or Simpson's, although this time the line was a telephone line. Just select the desired items from the catalogue, pick up the phone, call the order department for Eaton's or Simpson's, place the order and then sit back and wait for the stuff to appear right at your front door. In fact, when ordering from either of these two stores, a quick glance up the street when the horse-drawn wagon turned the corner would quickly tell you if your order was on its way. That's because if you ordered from Eaton's and it was a dapple grey in front of the approaching wagon, you could go back inside. Those dapple greys pulled Simpson wagons. What you wanted was a horse of a different colour. Eaton's preferred the chestnuts.

"Goods Satisfactory or Money Refunded"

This famous guarantee comes from Eaton's Catalogue and was once a byword in households across the country. The T. Eaton Co. was founded by Irish Immigrant Timothy Eaton in Toronto in 1869. The company's mail-order catalogue, sure to be found in most Canadian households, was issued annually from 1884 to 1976.

Indigo Book and Music Cafe, one of 300 stores in Toronto's top "tourist" attraction, the Eaton Centre. The Eaton family declared bankruptcy in 1997 and today the existing Eaton stores are owned and operated by Sears.

A Simpson delivery wagon drawn by a pair of dapple greys poses for the photographer in front of the Dalhousie Street truck garage, c1940.

J. Kendle & Company delivered coal from their yard on Van Horne Street (now part of Dupont Street) via a modern gasoline-powered truck.

The iceman cometh and it's coldeth. 1924.

Even the beer arrived by horse-drawn wagon like this one photographed on Victoria Street in downtown Toronto. Cosgrave's White Label Brewery was acquired by the famous E.P. Taylor in 1936.

Oakland Dairy, 110 Nassau Street in west central Toronto, was in the process of converting from oat-driven horse power to gasoline-driven horsepower when this photograph was taken in 1928. The era of most horse-drawn vehicles came to an end in the 1930s, however some companies gave their steeds a new lease on life when the WW 2 prompted severe gas rationing.

A Weston bread wagon blocks part of Lewis Street in east central Toronto as the salesman makes his deliveries, 1951.

George Weston opened his first bakery on Sullivan Street in 1885. He was the namesake of the modern George Weston Limited, a huge Canadian enterprise that is engaged in the wholesale and retail distribution of food and other products.

Interior of Michie's Grocery at the corner of King and Yonge c.1910.

Interior of Loblaws store on Queen's Quay East today. Photo courtesy: Loblaws Supermarkets.

LOBLAWS

For most people, the names of the places were they do their shopping mean little if anything. Eaton's is a just another word for department store while Zehr's means discount department store. Reitman's is simply the name of a ladies' clothing store while Mappins stands for jewellery store. Harvey's is synonymous with hamburger and fries while Tim Horton's is a two word definition for a doughnut/cup of coffee combo. In fact, all of these business are named for real people. And all of them are Canadians. For Torontonians, perhaps the best known personality whose surname is now used interchangeably with the term supermarket is Theodore Loblaw. This farmer's son was born in Alliston, Ontario in 1873. At the age of 17, determined to improve his lot in life, he made his way to Toronto where he obtained employment in a small King Street East grocery store owned by W.G. Cork. Despite the fact that young Loblaw's pay was $3 a week, he managed to accumulate a nest egg of $800 with which he purchased part ownership of one of Cork's two stores. His partner was Cork's son Milton. By 1910, the two men oversaw 10 stores scattered throughout the city. These stores worked on the then unique "self serve" principle whereby the customer selected items from shelves and barrels and took them to a check-out counter. This lessened the number of staff required allowing the store to advertise "We Sell for Less". Nine years later Loblaw and Cork sold all 10 stores to another upstart grocery company. Those stores formed the nucleus of today's Dominion Store chain. But the two young men didn't retire from the grocery business. They opened another two stores in which they introduced the "cash and carry" principle. Now the customer not only did the work of selecting his/her requirements, but they paid cash then and there to boot. Obviously these ideas paid off handsomely since by 1929 there were 80 Loblaw stores, a name incidentally that could just as easily have been Cork's had Milton been the more flamboyant of the pair.

Loblaws Groceteria at 511 Davenport opened in 1921 and was closed in 1969.

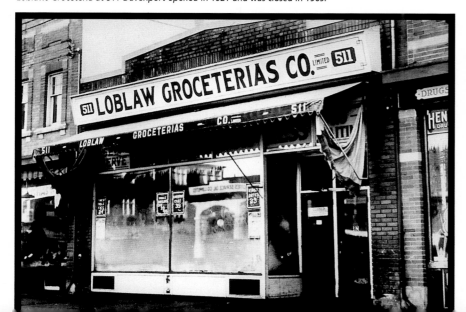

"When Americans visit Toronto they can't help noticing how darn nice the place is. It's so...clean. Hollywood movie crews import their own garbage to make Toronto streets look more like the good old USA And if they leave the rubbish unguarded, the city sweeps it up."

Rick Marin
Television columnist for The Washington Times and former Torontonian.

"Honest Ed's, crazy Honest Ed's"

This was part of a very well-known
radio jingle that Ed used for years.

*The original "Honest Ed's" (below) was located in this converted house at the southeast corner of Bloor and Markham streets. This photograph was taken in 1954, the same year that the term "Honest Ed's" was used for the first time."
The old house is still part of today's greatly enlarged "Honest Ed's", a fixture at the busy corner of Bloor and Bathurst.*

"Honest Ed's" is a place that's difficult to describe. You really have to go there to understand what it's all about. In fact, "Honest Ed's" discount department store has become so popular that it now ranks as one of the city's most popular tourist attractions, right up there with the Eaton Centre (which it's a little like) and the Zoo (which it's a lot like). The "Ed's" part, as any Torontonian will tell you, refers to legendary entrepreneur Ed Mirvish who, along with his wife Anne, has operated some form of retail outlet on Bloor Street since the days of WW 2. First came a small dress shop, then a fearsome mortgage and the "Famous Bargain House". We jump ahead to 1954, a very busy year in Toronto during which Torontonians got to ride the city's first subway, a 16-year-old local schoolgirl named Marilyn Bell won the hearts of all Canadians when she became the first person to swim across Lake Ontario and mean old Hurricane Hazel laid waste to many areas of the city. And the "Famous Bargain House" on Bloor street got a new name. It became "Honest Ed's."

Britnell's was the book lover's book store. Established in 1893 by Albert Britnell, a recent arrival from Yorkshire, England, to a still somewhat backwater Toronto, the original Britnell's Book Shop was located on lower Yonge Street. Here it remained until a move was made some years later to a new address, still on Yonge Street mind you, but now in the north end of town, a few steps north of the still sane Bloor Street intersection. Right up until the end came in 1999, Britnell's remained a class act. It's passing evoked sadness.

A modern Chapters book store, Bloor Street west of Yonge. Like the new style of shopping malls made up entirely of the so called "big box stores", book-selling in the '90s underwent a revolution with the advent of Chapters and Indigo. Not only could customers sit in comfortable armchairs to preview their purchases - or simply read them, drink their coffee and depart - they could also stay home and order on-line. In the very near future it will also be possible to download many titles directly to your computer's printer. Interesting times!

View east along Scarborough's Eglinton Avenue from its western terminus at Victoria Park, shortly before the Township purchased much of the land (seen in this 1949 photo) from the Federal Government . Eglinton Avenue in Scarborough was connected to the Eglinton Avenue in the city 7 years later, one of the first projects undertaken by the new Metro Toronto government.

View east along Eglinton Avenue from Victoria Park in 1955 showing the original Golden Mile shopping centre in its second year of operation.

GOLDEN MILE OF INDUSTRY

In 1948, Oliver Crockford, reeve of the land-rich Township of Scarborough, convinced his skeptical council it was worthwhile to purchase 89 hectares (220 acres) of land bordering Eglinton Avenue made surplus by the closure of a plant that had manufactured shell fuzes during the war. He later convinced them to augment this purchase when the nearby 73-hectare (180-acre) Harris Estate came onto the market.

And Crockford's instincts were right. No sooner had the ink on the paper dried than land-hungry industries appeared, eager to buy a parcel and set up shop on what was to become the "Golden Mile of Industry." First came Frigidaire, then SKF, quickly followed by Link Belt, Rootes and many others. Then Principal Investments added Canada's largest shopping centre, which would ultimately boast 35 stores, a 24-lane bowling alley, a 1000-seat theatre and free parking for 2000 vehicles. Five years after it opened to a bedazzled public in April 1954, Queen Elizabeth herself broke from her planned itinerary in Toronto for an impromptu visit to the famed Golden Mile Plaza. By the mid-1980s, however, even larger shopping malls had enticed customers elsewhere and the history-making complex at the northeast corner of Eglinton and Victoria Park was demolished, to be replaced by the latest in shopping technology, the supercentre.

View east along Eglinton Avenue from Victoria Park. Huge super stores now stand on what was the once-spectacular Golden Mile Plaza site on the north side of Eglinton. Eglinton Square shopping centre is on the south side of Eglinton.

View southeast to Highway 401 with the Dufferin and Allen interchanges, today. The intersection of Dufferin and Wilson is visible to the top left in this photo and Yorkdale Shopping Centre can be seen at top right.

Aerial view to the southeast over the intersection of Dufferin and Wilson in 1949.

Aerial view to the southeast showing Highway 401 and the Dufferin Street interchange in 1962. Yorkdale, Toronto's first regional shopping centre which opened in 1964 is under construction at the centre of the view.

View west to Sherway Gardens Shopping Centre with the Queen Elizabeth Way and Highway 427 interchange to the left and The Queensway to the right. The shopping centre opened in early 1971.

Sheppard Avenue East and Kennedy Road looking northwest. The sprawling Agincourt Mall is visible in the centre of the view and to the top right a portion of the municipally operated 18-hole, "pay as you play" Tam O'Shanter golf course.

Aerial view west along the Queen Elizabeth Way at Highway 427 in 1953.

Sheppard Ave. East and Kennedy Road looking northwest in 1949. Several sand traps of the then privately-owned Tam O'Shanter course on the northwest corner of the intersection are visible. This course was started in 1933. Over the years frontages were sold off for a variety of commercial uses. Finally, in 1973 what was left was purchased by the Metro Toronto, Scarborough and Ontario governments and is now the site of a smaller course and public park.

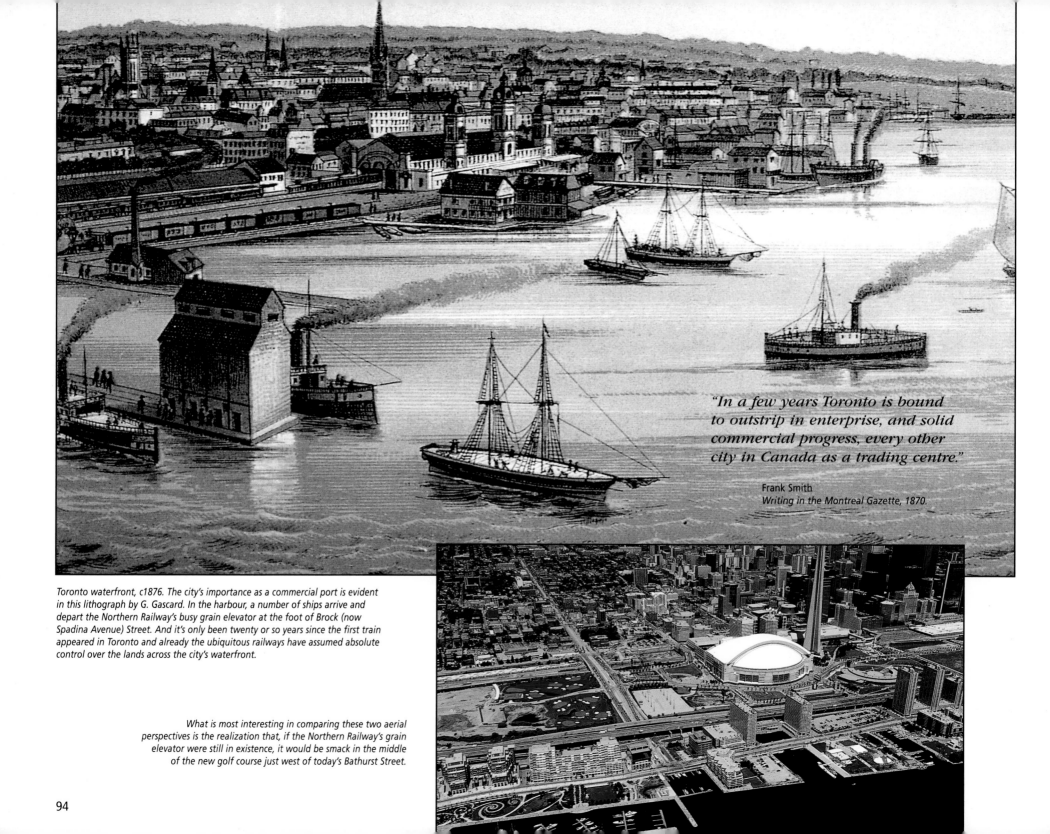

"*In a few years Toronto is bound to outstrip in enterprise, and solid commercial progress, every other city in Canada as a trading centre.*"

Frank Smith
Writing in the Montreal Gazette, 1870.

Toronto waterfront, c1876. The city's importance as a commercial port is evident in this lithograph by G. Gascard. In the harbour, a number of ships arrive and depart the Northern Railway's busy grain elevator at the foot of Brock (now Spadina Avenue) Street. And it's only been twenty or so years since the first train appeared in Toronto and already the ubiquitous railways have assumed absolute control over the lands across the city's waterfront.

What is most interesting in comparing these two aerial perspectives is the realization that, if the Northern Railway's grain elevator were still in existence, it would be smack in the middle of the new golf course just west of today's Bathurst Street.

The Yonge Street Slip, c1926. The buildings in the distance still stand but are now hidden from view by a multitude of modern skyscrapers.

Yonge Street Slip. The Toronto Island ferry docks are in the foreground, adjacent to the Westin Harbour Castle Hotel which opened in 1975 on land reclaimed from Toronto Bay.

The Yonge Street Slip. This photograph was taken from the bow of the "M.V. Jadran", a former passenger liner on the Adriatic Sea which now serves as Captain John's floating restaurant. The Captain has been a landmark on Toronto's waterfront for more than three decades.

These photographs reflect about 75 years of development around downtown Yonge Street.. Two buildings visible in both photos are the Public Building (west of Yonge Street and just north of the railway tracks) and peeping out behind it, the lovely old Bank of Montreal, since 1993 home to the Hockey Hall of Fame.

YONGE STREET

YONGE STREET IS TORONTO'S PRINCIPAL THOROUGHFARE AND REFLECTS THE CITY'S VIBRANCY. THE LONGEST STREET IN THE WORLD (ACCORDING TO THE GUINESS BOOK OF WORLD RECORDS) BEGINS AT TORONTO HARBOUR, RUNS NORTH THROUGH THE CITY, THEN PASSES THROUGH NUMEROUS ONTARIO TOWNS ALL THE WAY TO RAINY RIVER, ONTARIO, AND INTERNATIONAL FALLS IN MINNESOTA AT THE US BORDER. TOTAL DISTANCE IS **1,896** KM (**1,178** MILES.)

King Street looking east at Yonge Street, 1897. The streetcars are decorated in honour of the 60th anniversary of Queen Victoria's ascension to the throne.

Yonge Street looking north to the King Street corner, 1914. That this is the heyday of the streetcar is evident when, with a sharp eye, it is possible to count 22 of them up to Dundas Street. And sharp eyes may already have picked out the gent having his lunch about 50 feet above the sidewalk on the ledge of the newly completed Royal Bank building (light coloured structure at centre-right). While you're at it, can you find the old Globe newspaper sign and the CNE banner? It is interesting to note that the banner is advertising that the major grandstand spectacular would be the "Peace Year Tatoo" even though the war wouldn't end for another 4 years. That was because everyone, including the CNE promotion department, thought the war would be over by Christmas that year. How wrong they were.

Yonge and Richmond streets today. When completed in 1892, the Confederation Life Building at the northeast corner of Yonge and Richmond streets was the largest office building in Canada.

"I was born in "Toronto the Good," and as it became less good - it got better!"

Sam Sniderman

Looking south on Yonge to Richmond Street today.

Yonge Street north of Queen Street, 1887.

Yonge looking north at Queen Street, 1941.

At first, Yonge Street was not even part of the town. John Graves Simcoe, then provincial governor of Upper Canada – and founder of the city – had the initial portion of the road built (north of the town) in 1796 in anticipation of an American invasion; the road would assure military access to and from the northern Great Lakes. This was of strategic importance if the Americans ever managed to control the southern Lakes. The street itself was named in honour of his friend and one-time fellow parliamentarian Sir George Yonge, who at the time served as Secretary of War in the cabinet of King George III.

Northeast corner Yonge and King streets, c1912.

Northeast corner Yonge and King today.

During the 1800s, Yonge Street reached the edge of Lake Ontario and became the main thoroughfare for traders, farmers, militia and stage coach passengers entering and leaving the city. By 1850, there were only two large estates on Yonge between College and Bloor. Land grants of 200 acres (with a quarter of a mile of frontage) made Yonge a thoroughfare mostly lined with forests. In 1869, Timothy Eaton revolutionized Canadian shopping with his department store at 178 Yonge Street. This attracted other merchants, and by the early 1900s Yonge had become Toronto's premiere shopping street.

Today, the street (between King and Bloor) is filled with shoppers, commuters, young people cruising "the strip", theatre-goers and anybody who's simply interested in soaking up the atmosphere. But as soon as you leave the downtown core, Yonge takes on a whole new personality, or better still, personalities: from a strange mix of quality stores next to shops with garish neon lights and tacky window displays at Dundas, to the quaint antique stores in Rosedale, to the trendy cafes at Eglinton Avenue, all the way up to the strip malls of Richmond Hill. And then it travels further north on its journey as the world's longest street and, as in Toronto, becomes the main thoroughfare in the many towns and villages through which it ran. (Courtesy Tourism Toronto)

Three intriguing views c.1876 looking west on King from Yonge (top), south on Yonge from King (middle), and north on Yonge from King (bottom). Judging from the light and absence of activity, it is probably a weekend morning. Perhaps it is a Saturday and everyone is over at the St. Lawrence Market.

Aerial view of Yonge and Bloor streets looking to the north west in 1956.

YONGE AND BLOOR

As the pioneer surveyors began laying out the various roads in and around the young City of Toronto, officials found it necessary to devise a method of providing funds for the ongoing upkeep of what were nothing more than dirt paths that frequently became impassable during periods of inclement weather. The most obvious answer was tolls. Yonge Street, being one of the busiest highways in the county at the time, was a prime target. Tolls, which were first levied in the early 1830s, ranged from a penny per animal to several pennies for each vehicle. Toll gates were soon erected just north of what is now known as the crossroads of the city and accounts for the fact that ever-fashionable Bloor Street was originally named Toll-gate Road. Virtually all toll roads in the province were eliminated in 1896 never to return, officials vowed. Provincial taxes on income and gasoline would look after the problem. But toll roads have staged a come-back in 1997 with the opening of Highway 407 (now dubbed an ETR, "electronic toll road").

Aerial view of Yonge and Bloor streets looking to the north west.
Yonge runs diagonally from bottom left to top right.

Yonge Street looking north across Bloor c.1955 and today.

St. Clair Avenue looking west across Yonge Street c.1910 and today.

St. Clair Avenue looking east from Bathurst Street c.1910 and today. Imagine if the young lady on the boardwalk could be time-transported to this same spot in the contemporary photo.

Yonge Street looking north to St. Clair Avenue, 1912.

Toronto Railway Company streetcar passes Timothy Eaton Memorial Church, St. Clair Avenue West, in 1915.

Toronto Transportation Commission streetcar passes the same church 42 years later, 1957.

St. Clair Avenue was originally called the Third Concession Road being exactly the length of one concession north of the Second Concession Road known variously as the Toll-gate Road, St.Paul's Road (after nearby St. Paul's Anglican Church) and the present Bloor Street. It's believed that the St. Clair title was taken from a character in "Uncle Tom's Cabin", a very popular novel at the time the area in and around Yonge and St. Clair was first being settled.

Toronto Transit Commission streetcar passing the same church today.

Two little girls dressed up in their Easter finery posing on the wooden sidewalk at Yonge & Eglinton, 1922.

Automobile motoring north on Yonge near Eglinton, 1917.

North west corner of Yonge and Eglinton today.

Two views north on Yonge at Eglinton in 1917 and today. In the lovely old image a Toronto Police Constable is talking with the local garbage collector.

The dramatic change reflected in these two photographs is really most evident in the twenty year period from 1906 to 1926 (two black & white photos). For here we see evidence of an early housing boom as a pine tree-lined dirt path delineates' what would soon become Glengrove Avenue West with its row of stately homes. And the real drama of the contemporary image is the remarkable 75-year stability of the street. The only difference we see is the change from coniferous to deciduous trees.

While the privately-owned Toronto Street Railway was busy handling the travelling public's needs within the city proper, a separate company was established in 1877 to serve the communities that had sprung up along Yonge Street north of the city. As the years passed, business increased so that by 1909 electric streetcar service (now dubbed "radials" because they radiated out from the city core) had reached Sutton on Lake Simcoe.

One of the most popular destinations along the Metropolitan route was a pleasure ground at the end of a long line of pine trees that ran westerly from a Metropolitan streetcar stop that quickly took the name of the park, Glen Grove. In addition to a baseball grounds and picnic grove there was a race course. Frequently, during the summer months, a collection of a half-dozen or so streetcars would lay over at the Glen Grove stop waiting the return of hundreds who were spending the afternoon watching "the sport of kings."

"Real Torontonians wish they were living in the City of North York."

Mel Lastman 1984
At the time, Mel Lastman was mayor of North York.
He went on to become a colourful and popular mayor of a new, larger Toronto that was

Aerial view of the busy Yonge and Finch intersection looking to the north west. Yonge Street crosses this view from lower left to middle right. Post-war housing clearly visible in the archival view (at lower left, opposite page) is almost completely hidden beneath the trees that have grown up in the half century that has passed between the two images.

Aerial view looking north east to Yonge Street between Sheppard and Finch. The North York Civic Centre and Mel Lastman Square, which front onto the west side of Yonge Street just south of Finch Avenue, can be seen in this photograph. To the west of this complex is York Cemetery which had its first interments in the mid-1940s.

As Toronto grew after the WW 2, many young families and newcomers moved out to take advantage of cheaper properties in the rural areas surrounding the city. A few of the houses in this north Yonge Street neighborhood still survive despite the pressures of development on the Yonge Street corridor. As a direct result of those pressures and the extension of the Yonge subway to Finch in 1974, many of these houses have been swallowed up by office, apartment and condominium towers.

Aerial view of the Yonge and Finch area looking to the north west in the late 1940s. Finch Avenue runs off to the west (top center) and the actual Yonge & Finch intersection is outside the frame to the bottom right of this view.

Aerial view looking north east to Yonge Street between Sheppard and Finch. Evident in this c.1930 photo is the old (and in this view abandoned) Willowdale Airfield on which York Cemetery was to be laid out in the mid-1930s. Also visible in this and the above photograph is the Michael Sheppard House built in 1843 by a member of the family for whom Sheppard Avenue was named. The house is now used as an office by cemetery staff.

York University looking south towards downtown Toronto today.

Future site of York University looking south over farmland towards Downsview Airport and downtown Toronto in 1958. Note that in both views we see the same large grove of trees (foreground, left of centre), runways at Downsview Airport (background, left of centre) and (top left) a group of fuel storage tanks on Finch Avenue.

YORK UNIVERSITY

York University was established in 1959 and for the first few years of its existence classes were held at the University of Toronto's Falconer Hall and then in existing buildings at a former U of T campus, Glendon Hall on Bayview Avenue. Enrolment continued to increase at a rapid rate and soon officials found it necessary to acquire a site where ongoing expansion could be accommodated. The site selected at the southwest corner of Steeles Avenue West and Keele Street was originally the farm of Jacob Stong. Even when work on the new campus began in the early 1960s, the area was still dotted with a multitude of farm fields. York University opened at its new 243 hectare campus in 1965. Today, the university (which operates three sites, North York, Glendon and a downtown management centre) offers nearly 5,000 courses per year, boasts nearly 34,000 undergraduate students, 4,100 graduate students and an alumni totalling more than 150,000.

"A sense of wonder is in itself a religious feeling. But in so many people the sense of wonder gets lost. It gets scarred over. It is as though a tortoise shell has grown over it. People reach a stage where they're never surprised, never delighted. They're never suddenly aware of glorious freedom or splendour in their lives. However hard a life may be, I think for virtually all people this is possible."

Robertson Davies

115

Half Way House at its original location on Kingston Road at Midland c.1900.

Half Way House in all its restored splendor.

Roblin Mill

BLACK CREEK PIONEER VILLAGE

TORONTO'S DEADLIEST STORM, HURRICANE HAZEL, WITH A LITTLE HELP FROM ELIZABETH ARDEN, HEAD OF THE GLOBAL COSMETICS COMPANY, SPAWNED ONE OF THE CITY'S MOST BELOVED FAMILY ATTRACTIONS, BLACK CREEK PIONEER VILLAGE.

Hurricane Hazel was born near the island of Grenada in the Caribbean on October 5, 1954, and as she progressed northward, weather experts predicted that the massive storm would follow the usual track, keeping Hazel well away from populated centres around the Great Lakes. However, the experts were wrong. Hazel struck the North American continent near Myrtle Beach, South Carolina, curved northward, ravaged Washington, D.C. and then made straight for Lake Ontario, blasting the north shore and the city of Toronto shortly after 11:00 p.m. on Friday, October 15. Within 24 hours, 183 mm (7.2 in.) of rain – that's more than 300 tons of water –

fell on a city already waterlogged by a series of downpours earlier in the month. Damage in excess of $100 million resulted and over 90 lives were lost, including 36 on one street that was simply washed away by the usually gentle Humber River. As the flood waters receded, government officials began to make plans to ensure that such destruction might be diminished in the event of another similar blast by Mother Nature. One of the first steps taken was the acquisition of 5.7 hectares (14 acres) of flood plain land at the northwest corner of Jane Street and Steeles Avenue astride a tributary of the Humber River known as Black Creek.

Laskay's Emporium and Post Office as it appeared in 1960.

Laskay's Emporium and Post Office 40 years later.

Wedding party passing the Tinsmith Shop on their way to the reception.

Just three weeks before Hazel struck, Elizabeth Arden, a pioneer in the field of cosmetics and advertising, had participated in the official opening of the Dalziel Pioneer Park on these very same flood plain lands. Arden had lived on the property until she was 24 years of age, no doubt often helping her father, a tenant farmer, around the ancient barn erected in 1809 for the homesteading Dalziel family. By the time she opened the heritage park, however, Arden had become one of the richest women in America, earning more money per year than any other woman in U.S. history, according to an early edition of Fortune magazine.

A neighbouring pioneer farm, the Daniel Stong property, was added to the flood plain acquisition four years later, bringing with it two log houses, a piggery, a barn and remnants of several other out buildings all of which date back to the early 1800s. On June 2, 1960, the combined properties opened to the public as Black Creek Pioneer Village, a living museum that demonstrates life in rural Canada in the 1860s. Over the years, many "orphaned" structures such as the Roblin Mill, Half Way House and the Laskay Emporium were moved to the 22.6-hectare (56-acre) site that now boasts more than 35 homes, workshops, public buildings and farm buildings and where artisans and farmhands bring to life once again the forgotten skills of 19th century rural daily life.

"Good rich forest land can be bought within a day's journey of Toronto, the capital of Upper Canada, with a population of 16,000, for twelve dollars per acre."

William Thompson
Traveler and writer, 1840.

Group portrait of Victorian era constables posing in front of Police Staion No. 4 at Wilton (Dundas) and Parliament, 1888.

POLICE DEPARTMENT

THE ANXIOUS COP DID WHAT EVERY COP DOES WHEN HE IS IN TROUBLE, HE REACHED INTO HIS POCKET AND PULLED OUT – A BIG BRASS KEY. THE YEAR WAS 1888 AND 60 POLICE CALL BOXES HAD JUST BEEN INSTALLED ACROSS THE CITY. WHEN THE KEY WAS INSERTED INTO ONE OF TWO KEYHOLES ON THE OUTSIDE OF A BOX, THE LOCAL POLICE STATION WAS AUTOMATICALLY ALERTED THAT THE BEAT OFFICER NEEDED HELP. THE SECOND KEYHOLE WOULD GIVE HIM ACCESS TO A TELEPHONE AND MESSAGE PAD INSIDE THE BOX. IT IS TO BE HOPED THAT THE UNNERVED OFFICER CHOOSES THE RIGHT KEYHOLE IN HIS MOMENT OF NEED.

Police call boxes remained familiar urban fixtures until the 1970s, when radios and computers sent them the way of the dinosaur as communication tools. However, for 80 years, they provided an effective method of contact between the officer on the street and home base. When the sergeant wanted to pass along a message, a red light would flash on top of the box – one flash for a message intended only for the beat constable, two for all officers, and three for an emergency. Before this marvellous technology, a passing pedestrian was the only hope of communication between the station and the officer on the street.

Until 1834, when Toronto officially received city status, the peace was maintained by one voluntary High Constable – a position of some status – and however many unpaid assistants were deemed necessary at a given time. With incorporation, the city hired five full time officers at an annual salary of $150 each. They were augmented by the availability of 14 Special Constables who could be called upon if and when needed – and in a rapidly expanding city with a population already topping 9250 residents, no doubt the need was frequent. Thirty-five years later, the force had increased to a total of 59 full time officers serving a population now numbering almost 47,000.

The city's first officers faced many challenges in 1834. Stopping speeding horses was one of them, keeping in mind that Toronto's mounted unit was not introduced until 1886. Diverting cattle drives from the city's main thoroughfare, Yonge Street, was another, along with apprehending shop keepers who insisted on dumping their garbage onto that same street, to the discomfort of passing pedestrians. (Fortunately for the patrolling officers, Yonge Street had not yet stretched northwest to its full 1896-kilometre (1178-mile) length, making it the longest street in the world.) They also had to deal with illegal liquor sales, illegal swimming in Lake Ontario and illegal activities on the Sabbath Day – which was just about any activity other than worship and rest.

Constable using one of the call boxes, the major communications device for almost 75 years.

Traffic Officer in action at Yonge and Queen, c.1912.

In 1876, the life of a Toronto police officer took a decided turn for the better. A Class 'A' constable with more than 10 years on the job saw his pay increasing to $1.90 a day while the daily wage for sergeants and detectives rose to $2.55 and, for inspectors, a whopping $2.90. Constables also got ten days annual holiday with pay, senior ranks two weeks. Uniforms were provided (one a year), as were handcuffs and a revolver. In addition, the city was now to be patrolled all night long and not left unattended from four in the morning until nine, as in the past. Bicycles for patrols were introduced in 1894, fingerprinting eased criminal identification after 1906, the first parking ticket was issued in 1907, motorcycles speeded response time in 1911, and the following year the traffic branch was created. In 1913, the first female police officer was hired (though pay equity didn't come along until 1945), in 1938 two-way radios came into use, and in 1989 the force was fortified by the work of trained police dogs.

But it was an elephant, a fictional elephant, which perhaps did most to create the positive relationship that exists today between the city's 2.4 million residents and the $522-million-a-year police force's 4904 uniform officers and 238 auxiliaries (who continue the volunteer tradition begun in 1834). The community's youngest citizens were introduced in elementary school to Elmer the Safety Elephant – and to his "keeper," the friendly local constable. Such a positive introduction to law enforcement at such an early age is no doubt part of the reason the city experienced a decrease in criminal offences of all kinds, as "Elmer's children" grow up and take their place in society. It's little wonder, then, that the largest single policing unit in Canada's most populous city is the Traffic Squad.

Constables during inspection in front of No. 1 Station on Court Street, c.1925.

Traffic Squad Officers c.1950.

Officers on bicycle patrol in front of 52 Division on Dundas Street West.

Officer preparing for her patrol at 52 Division on Dundas Street West.

FIRE DEPARTMENT

"THERE'S GOOD NEWS AND THERE'S BAD NEWS," THAT'S WHAT THE LEADER PROBABLY TOLD HIS SQUADRON OF VOLUNTEER FIREMEN — SOME OF THE CITY'S MOST INFLUENTIAL BUSINESSMEN — BACK IN 1826 UPON THE ARRIVAL OF THE COMMUNITY'S LONG-ANTICIPATED FIRST PIECE OF FIRE FIGHTING EQUIPMENT, A "GOOSE NECK" PUMPER. THE GOOD NEWS WAS: IT WOULD WORK BETTER THAN THE OLD-FASHIONED BUCKET BRIGADE. THE BAD NEWS WAS: THEY'D HAVE TO USE THEIR OWN BRUTE FORCE — INFLUENTIAL OR NOT — TO HAUL THE HEAVY PIECE OF MACHINERY ALL THE WAY FROM THE CITY'S ONLY FIREHALL, LOCATED ON CHURCH STREET BETWEEN COURT AND ADELAIDE, TO THE SITE OF THE BLAZE, HOWEVER FAR AWAY THAT MIGHT BE.

But it was worth the effort. Once at the fire, eight men positioned themselves along each side of the proudly christened "York" and pumped long side bars to project a stream of water a distance of some 42 metres (140 feet). Previously, they had relied solely on residents complying with a bylaw that required each householder to hang two leather buckets full of water in a conspicuous place in front of their homes. Then, when a fire was detected, the bell in the steeple of St. James' Church (the only bell in town) would be rung and a double row of citizens would form between the waterfront or the nearest cistern and the burning building. Starting with the buckets hanging outside nearby houses, full buckets would pass along one side of the line towards the fire and empty buckets would return to the water source via the other. This elementary firefighting method was effective, sometimes. More often, however, it was not.

The "York", of course, was only useful when there was a goodly quantity of water available. When the alarm was sounded, several freelance carters would immediately race to the scene of the fire with horse-drawn wagons on which large 150-225 litre (40-60 gallon) casks of

water had been mounted. However, in their haste to receive the top payment of $4.00 by being the first to arrive — the next three received only $3.00, $2.00 and $1.00 respectively — the frantic dash over rough roads often resulted in the casks being close to empty when the carters got to the blaze.

The next major improvement in the city's fire fighting capabilities occurred in 1861 when the first two steam fire engines were purchased for $6000 from Sisby and Company in Seneca Falls, New York. At first, the budget didn't allow for horses to pull the new engines and so, when the alarm was rung, the firemen simply commandeered whatever steeds were near at hand and off they went. In 1874, when City Council replaced the volunteer force with a permanent brigade of fifty men and an annual budget of less than $35,000, there still was not enough money for horses and so they were merely contracted into service on an "as needed" basis. Finally, in 1890, 74 years after the first firemen allowed themselves to serve as draft horses for the York, the city at last coughed up $4630 for 28 specimens of the real thing. The department's last pair of precious horses, Mickey and Prince, were retired with great ceremony in 1931.

A quartette of Toronto firemen pose with two of the department's most modern pieces of equipment, a hose reel and steam engine c1885.

Town of North Toronto volunteer firemen pose outside the department's #5 Fire Hall, c1910. With many of the community's residences made of wood and lit with kerosene lamps the firemen were certainly kept busy.

Firemen stationed at department headquarters on Adelaide Street West pose for the camera c. 1930.

The firemen's tradition of pride in their skills and equipment is reflected in the contemporary photos of some of the men stationed at Firehall No. 5 on Front Street East and No. 9 on Queen's Quay West.

Members of today's Toronto Fire Service do a lot more than fight fires. They are also experts at vehicle extrication, fire prevention and emergency preparedness and devote a lot of time to instructing the community on home safety. The department's 3100 personnel operate out of 80 fire halls and have at their disposal the fireboat William Lyon Mackenzie (named for Toronto's first mayor) and 135 other firefighting vehicles – all of them, fortunately, motorized!

1904 FIRE

The evening of April 19, 1904 was cold and raw. A stiff wind was blowing from the northwest and there was snow in the air. Shortly after 8pm a patrolling constable spotted flames shooting from an upper window at the Currie neckwear factory at 58 Wellington Street West, a few doors west of Bay. An alarm was immediately turned in and within minutes the first firemen appeared on the scene. But it quickly became evident that this was not to be an ordinary fire. In the short time it had taken crews to respond, the flames had leapt to nearby buildings and now the entire corner was engulfed. Try as they might to contain the fire, the wind and the lack of water pressure in the city's antiquated fire fighting mains and hydrants were against them. The fire continued to spread and soon dozens of buildings were fully involved. A call went out for assistance and in short order men and equipment from as far away as Hamilton and Buffalo, New York were on the job. In total, 230 firemen with five steam pumpers, 15 hose wagons and two water towers fought the conflagration, which at its peak had consumed virtually every building in the heart of the city as well as a number of wharves and warehouses along the waterfront.

View north along Bay Street the day after the disasterous fire. Through the smoke the clock tower of City Hall on Queen Street West can be seen at the top of the street.

Front Street looking east to the Bay Street corner after the fire.

Bay Street looking north to City Hall in 1900. This is what Bay Street looked like prior to the fire.

View north on Bay Street today. Improved building codes along with modern fire fighting equipment and techniques makes the possibilty of a similar disaster unlikely. But, some say, not impossible.

The fire was finally brought under control late in the afternoon of the following day. Miraculously, no one died in the inferno though injuries were numerous. Over the following weeks, hot spots continued to flare and it took additional weeks before insurance adjusters could inspect the site and provide an anxious city with estimates of the damage it had suffered. When the figures were released they confirmed that more than 100 buildings had been destroyed or badly damaged in a catastrophe that affected nearly 140 businesses, throwing more than 6,000 people out of work. Property loss exceeded ten million (1904) dollars and there was some doubt that the city could even survive the incredible amount of destruction that had been inflicted by the worst fire in its history.

"If Montreal is a city of heritage and Vancouver a city of style, Toronto is a city of influence."

Peter C. Newman

Galleria of BCE Place looking east from the Bay Street entrance. The old Commercial Bank of the Midland District, visible in its original setting opposite, was artfully incorporated into the design of this complex. To accomplish this, the old building was taken apart stone by stone, the stones numbered and stored and later re-assembled.

The Commercial Bank of the Midland District in its original location at 15 Wellington Street, just west of Yonge, c.1880. After a number of changes of ownership, the Commercial Bank was finally absorbed by the Bank of Montreal in 1922.

THE BANKS

M-I-N-T. CLEAR AS DAY, FOR THOSE WHO WOULD SEE IT, THE ANNOUNCEMENT OF TORONTO'S STATUS AS THE FINANCIAL HEART OF CANADA IS SPELLED OUT, LITERALLY, ON THE FOUR CORNERS OF THE INTERSECTION OF KING AND BAY STREETS AT THE CORE OF THE CITY'S BUSTLING FINANCIAL SECTOR. THE MONTREAL. THE IMPERIAL (COMMERCE). THE NOVA SCOTIA. AND THE TORONTO DOMINION. COMBINED, THESE INSTITUTIONS REPRESENT 80 PER CENT OF THE COUNTRY'S MAJOR DOMESTIC BANKS, THE LARGEST CORPORATIONS IN CANADA. AND IF THE ARTFULNESS OF THAT ACRONYMISTIC EVIDENCE IS TOO SUBTLE, THERE IS ALWAYS THE IMPOSSIBLE-TO-MISS DOMINATION OF THE AREA BY THE TOWERING AND MAJESTIC OFFICE BLOCKS THAT REPRESENT THESE BANKS, ONE ON EACH OF THE INTERSECTION'S FOUR CORNERS. THEN, JUST A SHORT STROLL DOWN BAY STREET TO FRONT STREET, THERE IS THE DAZZLING GOLDEN SKYSCRAPER OF THE ROYAL, CANADA'S LARGEST CHARTERED BANK.

Aerial view of downtown core looking south west towards the "M-I-N-T" concentration of bank towers that - along with the CN Tower - so define Toronto's skyline. Lower Bay Street has long been regarded as the financial heart of the city, imposing. Here's why: (left to right) the Royal Bank Plaza (once described as looking like God's chandelier that had fallen from heaven), Commerce Court (the old Bank of Commerce in the foreground), the T-D Centre, Scotia Plaza and First Canadian Place (head office of the Bank of Montreal and the tallest office building in the country). Overlooking them all is the ubiquitous CN Tower.

"Ant's eye" view of the bank towers at the corner of King and Bay streets. Counter clockwise from lower left we see; First Canadian Place, Scotia Plaza, Commerce Court and the T-D Centre.

But it wasn't always this way. In 1819, Kingston, the economic satellite of booming Montreal and home to three of the most successful private banks in existence at the time, was ahead of the game. Then the colonial government announced the charter for the new Bank of Upper Canada and eager businessmen from both Kingston and York put in their bids. It was the upstart, York, that won. In hindsight, this outcome was inevitable, given that many of the prospective bankers were members of the legislature located in York, or these legislators were neighbours and associates of the town's would-be bankers. Thus the seeds were sown for Toronto, the centre of government, to become Toronto, the centre of business and finance. In addition to being home today to the executive offices of most of Canada's major financial institutions, 46 of the 55 foreign banks operating in the nation have also chosen to locate their head offices in the city.

Bird's eye view of those same bank towers above the intersection of King and Bay streets. The 72-storey First Canadian Place (left) on the northwest corner was completed in 1979 and at 290 meters (952 feet) is the tallest office building in Canada. Scotia Plaza (right,) at the northeast corner of the same intersection, is 275 meters (902 feet) high and was completed in 1988.

Toronto Stock Exchange building at 234 Bay Street, 1972.
Photo: Larry Milberry

The Design Exchange has taken over the premises vacated by the TSE in 1983 and the old building has been artfully incorporated into the newer Toronto Dominion complex.

TORONTO STOCK EXCHANGE

THE TORONTO STOCK EXCHANGE, WHICH WAS ESTABLISHED IN 1852 BY 12 LOCAL GRAIN DEALERS AND WHOLESALERS, TODAY ACCOUNTS FOR 95 PER CENT OF ALL EQUITY TRADING IN CANADA. FROM TRADING TWICE EACH WEEKDAY AND AT NOON ON SATURDAYS IN FEWER THAN A DOZEN STOCKS BACK IN 1878, TODAY'S DAILY TSE TRADING HAS BEEN KNOWN TO TOP THE SIX BILLION DOLLAR MARK. IT IS CONSISTENTLY RANKED AS ONE OF THE WORLD'S TOP EXCHANGES, THE THIRD LARGEST BY VALUE AND SECOND LARGEST BY VOLUME ON THE NORTH AMERICAN CONTINENT. INDEED, BACK IN 1933 WHEN THOUSANDS OF AMERICAN EXCHANGES WERE FORCED TO FOLD UP AND DISAPPEAR, NO TSE MEMBER FIRM DEFAULTED ON ITS OBLIGATION TO CLIENTS. PERHAPS THIS IS TO BE EXPECTED FROM THE TYPE OF ORGANIZATION WHICH IN 1977 WAS ASTUTE ENOUGH TO LAUNCH THE WORLD'S FIRST COMPUTERIZED TRADING SYSTEM AND, IN 1999, TO APPOINT NORTH AMERICA'S FIRST FEMALE STOCK EXCHANGE PRESIDENT.

"Toronto, soul of Canada, is wealthy, busy, commercial, Scotch, absorbent of whisky."

Rupert Brooke
Writing in Letters from America, 1916.

Bay Street looking north from King Street, c1910. At top centre is the 90 meter (300 foot) high clock tower of City Hall. To its left is Toronto's first skyscraper, the mammoth 11-storey Temple Building at the Richmond Street corner.

Much has changed in this contemporary view north on Bay Street but the Clock Tower of the Old City Hall still stands on guard as proud witness to over 100 years of history.

131

Bay Street looking north to Richmond Street and City Hall, 1907.

View north on Bay Street at King. In this scene we see that a Moose - one of several hundred placed around the city as part of Toronto's Millennium celebrations - is challenging the 148 year supremacy of the Bulls and Bears of Bay Street.

TSE - HIGHLIGHTS

1852   Toronto's population is 32,000. The "Association of Brokers" is formed by 12 Toronto businessmen who begin to trade securities.

1901   Toronto's population is 208,040. Wilfrid Laurier is Prime Minister, Eatons sells eggs for 14 cents per dozen. The TSE moves to 20 King Street East. The number of stocks traded on the Exchange is now 200.

1933   More than 4.1 million Canadians are out of work as a result of the Great Depression. While nearly 2,000 investment and brokerage firms close their doors in the United States, no member firm of the TSE defaults on its obligation to clients.

1983   The TSE moves to First Canadian Place and The Exchange Tower.

2000   TSE monthly trading tops $100 billion for the first time ever in March 2000.

Toronto's prosperity emerged from its position as a centre of government, thus producing the professional elite that could support a more varied and affluent retail market than elsewhere in the province. These amenities attracted many migrants. By the turn of the 20th century the small workshops and individual craftsmen of the 1800s had given way to larger scale manufacturing – including textiles, wood products, paper, beer and soap. This unusually diverse manufacturing base attracted more migrants (Toronto was recently selected by the United Nations as the world's most multi-cultural, multi-ethnic city) and also allowed the city to weather economic fluctuations with a large degree of ease. A post-World War II decline in the manufacturing sector, due in part to the appeal of cheaper land outside the urban centre, did nothing to reverse the continuous, steady increase in the city's population as employment in service areas – such as retail, finance, insurance, real estate, business services, government services, education, health and social services – more than made up the difference. Today, Toronto is touted as being without parallel among North American metropolises, celebrated for its safety, its cleanliness and its high quality of life.

Noon hour traffic crowds Bay at Adelaide as Torontonians go about their last-minute shopping on December 24th, 1924.

"We stopped for some hours at Toronto, and had time to renew our acquaintance with that magnificent city, which seems to have taken to giddy ways, for she has erected an enormous glittering sort of Coney Island place along the lake-side, which was in full swing as we passed, with many thousands of people on swings and switchbacks and other diversions. If money paid to the saloons diminished the family standard, then it seems to me that these profitless excitements must have the same effect; yet it must be admitted that the monotony of modern economic life does call for some stimulant, if it be only taken in reason."

Sir Arthur Conan Doyle 1923

Aerial view of Lake Shore Boulevard and the Sunnyside Amusement Park after the 1949 season.

SUNNYSIDE

TODAY, WHEN TORONTONIANS WANT TO GET AWAY FROM IT ALL THEY USUALLY HEAD NORTH TO COTTAGE COUNTRY. IN THE CITY'S EARLY DAYS, HOWEVER, THEY'D HEAD WEST, ALL THE WAY OUT TO THE WOODED HINTERLAND ALONG THE NORTH SHORE OF LAKE ONTARIO BETWEEN THE YOUNG CITY AND THE STILL CLEAR AND FAST FLOWING WATERS OF THE HUMBER RIVER. THEY WERE OFF TO SUNNYSIDE.

As the outlying areas surrounding the fast growing City of Toronto began to develop, they quickly became unable to meet the demand for public amenities such as a dependable water supply, sewage facilities, garbage pick-up and the like. They petitioned the city to help them through annexation and the city obliged, taking into the fold 47 municipalities, farms and estates between 1883 and 1914. Sunnyside became part of Toronto in 1888. When the new Toronto Harbour Commission (THC) was created in 1911 it was authorized to bring some order to the chaos that had strangled the city's inner waterfront for decades. This included plans to improve the city's eastern and western beaches. Sunnyside was of particular interest to the commission for it would be here that a new boulevard highway would be built. This highway, in its final form, would encircle the city, including a stretch across Toronto Island complete with bridges over both the Eastern and Western channels. Rightly or wrongly, all that ever materialized from this far-sighted plan is that portion of the modern Lake Shore Boulevard between Bathurst Street and the Humber River.

Another component of the THC's western beach development scheme was the creation of a vast new bathing beach and the construction of an amusement park. The former would be created on land reclaimed from the old Humber Bay and dressed with huge quantities of fresh soil from Pickering Township east of the city. The play area would be complete with all the latest rides and games and a couple of dance halls, one of which, the Palais Royale is today awaiting a multi-million dollar facelift. It was hoped that these diversions would serve to attract not just the locals, but visitors from south of the border with their lovely American dollars. Sunnyside Amusement Park was officially opened in 1922 by Toronto mayor Alfred McGuire. Popularity of the park peaked during the depression and the Second World War when money became tight and the wonders of Sunnyside were just a 5 cent streetcar ride away.

But the times they were a-changin'. With the end of the war, cars and gasoline soon became plentiful and the desire to hit the open highway pushed such mundane attractions as Sunnyside to the back of the class. Soon many of these cars were clogging Lake Shore Boulevard and rumours of a new super highway destined to run right through the Park led to the inevitable closure of Sunnyside Amusement Park following the 1955 season. The first stretch of the new Gardiner Expressway opened less than three years later.

The Gardiner Expressway and Lake Shore Boulevard through Sunnyside, today.

The Sunnyside Bathing Pavilion, where visitors could change into suitable bathing attire, was frequently the site of major promotional activities such as this 1923 'Water Nymph Carnival' sponsored by the Toronto Evening Telegram newspaper.

Eager swimmers found the cold lake water refreshing in spite of the "Polluted Water" signs posted along the shoreline. Colder than normal summers in 1923 and 1924 resulted in the construction of a heated swimming pool next door to the pavilion which opened to the public the following year. In local circles it has always been known as "the tank". Although Officialdom christened this landmark the Sunnyside-Gus Ryder Pool, to locals it's still just "the tank".

The historic Sunnyside Bathing Pavilion, with its charming new café, is still a popular gathering place and one of the last remaining remnants of the famed old amusement park.

The roller coaster was called The Flyer and it traveled a million miles an hour. Rides such as the "Red Bug", "Whoopee", "Derby Racer" and "Gad-a-bout" were favourites with visitors to the park where the cool lake breezes filled one's head with the smell of Downyflake Donuts, candy apples and delicious Sunnyside red hots. Feet shuffled to the music of Ellis McLintock, Cy McLean, Harry Beddlington and others at dance halls such as the Palais Royale, the Seabreeze, the Club Esquire and the nearby Slipper and Palace Pier . And no other red hots could compare with those Sunnyside Red Hots.

Operating from Victoria Day to Labour Day for 34 wonderful years, civic officials ordered the park and amusements to be torn down in 1956. The main reason - traffic congestion!

Two young ladies posing for photograph at Toronto's other waterfront, Scarboro Beach in the city's east end.

THE HUMBER

From Toronto's earliest days, the route west along the shore of Lake Ontario to such distant points as Oakville, Hamilton and far-off Niagara has been of immense importance. Along the way there were major impediments, but none quite as difficult as the crossing of the Humber River. At first such crossings were made via a small ferry boat which was supplemented by a rickety wooden bridge some time around 1809. As the amount of traffic as well as the weight of the individual pieces of equipment using the structures increased, a series of larger and more substantial bridges became necessary. This need became even more critical with the completion of the Queen Elizabeth Highway to the city's western outskirts in the summer of 1940, followed by construction of The Queensway and the first phase of the new Gardiner Expressway in the mid-1950s. The rehabilitation and strengthening of existing bridges is ongoing. The newest structure to span the mouth of the watercourse is the attractive Humber River Pedestrian and Bicycle Bridge which opened to the public in late 1994.

An electric streetcar on the PORT CREDIT line has just crossed over the Mimico Creek bridge on the Lakeshore as it makes its way to the line's eastern terminus at Sunnyside. c1910.

A similar view today reflecting the endurance of the ubiquitous streetcar.

The Palace Pier dance hall is still standing in this late 1950s aerial photo of the Humber River bridges. When originally proposed in the 1920s, our Palace Pier was to be a larger version of the stately Palace Pier in Brighton, England. For a variety of reasons, mostly financial, only an abbreviated version was ever built which, unfortunately, went up in flames in early 1963.

A similar view in 2000 showing the new *Humber River Pedestrian and Bicycle Bridge and the Palace Pier and Palace Place condominium towers.*

SPORTS

THE EVOLUTION OF SPORTS IN CANADA FROM MERE PASTIMES INTO ORGANIZED CONTESTS WHERE ATHLETES WERE PAID TO DEMONSTRATE THEIR SKILLS AND FANS WILLINGLY PAID TO WATCH THEM WAS A DIRECT PRODUCT OF THE URBANIZATION THAT OCCURRED IN THE LATE 1800s AND EARLY 1900s. FOR THE FIRST TIME IN CANADIAN HISTORY, PEOPLE HAD SET WORKING HOURS, WHICH MEANT DEPENDABLE FREE TIME. THEY HAD STEADY MONEY, WHICH ALLOWED BUDGETING FOR RECREATION. THEY HAD THE ENTHUSIASM OF MANY LIKE-MINDED CLOSE NEIGHBOURS, WHICH INCREASED THE EXCITEMENT OF ROOTING FOR HOMETOWN TEAMS. AND THEY HAD THE COMBINED RESOURCES OF A LARGE COMMUNITY, WHICH ALLOWED THE CONSTRUCTION OF SPORTING FACILITIES BIG ENOUGH TO HOLD ALL OF THEIR FERVOUR AND FANATICISM. NOWHERE WAS THIS MORE EVIDENT THAN IN TORONTO. WHETHER YOU SLAPSHOT IT, PITCH IT, KICK IT, DUNK IT, PUTT IT, SERVE IT, BET ON IT OR SIMPLY CHEER IT, TORONTO HAS ALWAYS BEEN THE BEST PLACE TO FIND IT. INDEED, CANADA'S VERY FIRST WORLD CHAMPION SPORTSMAN HAILED FROM THE CITY — NED HANLAN WON THE WORLD TITLE FOR ROWING IN 1880 AND WENT ON TO SUCCESSFULLY DEFEND HIS CHAMPION STATUS A TOTAL OF SIX TIMES OVER THE NEXT FOUR YEARS.

SKYDOME

SKYDOME AND ITS NEXT DOOR NEIGHBOUR, THE CN TOWER, HAVE, TOGETHER, BECOME DEFINITIVE OF THE TORONTO SKYLINE THAT BORDERS THE SHORES OF LAKE ONTARIO. STARTING WITH THEIR COMMANDING PRESENCE, EVERYTHING ABOUT THESE STRUCTURES IS LARGER THAN LIFE.

The $600 million SkyDome – the world's first multiple purpose retractable dome stadium, whose name was selected from a list of 12,879 possibilities – is large enough to enclose a 31-storey skyscraper. Since its opening in 1989, it has spawned a number of would-be copycats elsewhere, but SkyDome remains ahead of the pack with the world's largest (three storeys high by nine storeys wide) display-screen-cum-scoreboard, the 92 metres long (300-foot) Sightlines lounge, and a major hotel in which one out of every five rooms overlooks the field of play. Indeed, hotel guests are reminded to close their drapes, should they

Long term plans call for the construction of numerous office and condominium towers, streets and parks on the lands to the west of SkyDome and the CN Tower. Until that project gets underway,

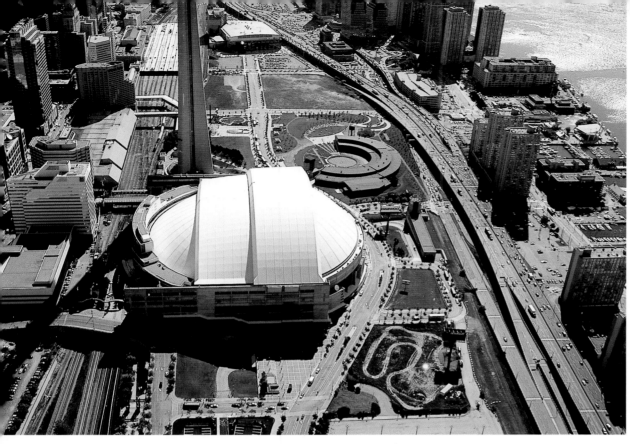

The four separate roof panels (numbered, from left to right, 1, 3, 4 and 2) are visible in this view of SkyDome. Section #1 is fixed in place, the other three move to expose 100% of the playing field and 90% of the interior. The new Air Canada Center, home to the Toronto Raptors, can be seen at the top centre.

decide to retire early, so as not to distract what could be over 65,000 spectators who have come to SkyDome to support their favourite sport, performer, trade show or convention.

Two major league sports teams call the behemoth home: the Canadian Football League's Toronto Argonauts and the American League's Toronto Blue Jays who, when they took the 1992 and 1993 World Series titles, forced American fans for the first time ever to procure a passport along with their World Series tickets. But SkyDome's attendance record was set on April Fool's Day 1990, when a total of 66,678 fans came out to cheer and jeer Wrestlemania VI.

The stadium was designed by local architect Rod Robbie. Robbie's structure incorporates an amazing retractable roof consisting of four panels, three moveable and one fixed, which can open or close completely within 20 minutes. The concept was conceived by Ottawa structural engineer Michael Allen while flying home after a meeting with Robbie at the latter's Toronto office. They wisely also incorporated into the building four times the number of women's comfort stations than men's, gaining an instant advantage over any other stadium in North America. Clearly, they understood how to advance the commercial success of their "secular cathedral" by pleasing the majority sector of Toronto's population.

BASKETBALL

THE CHALLENGE WAS TO CREATE A NEW INDOOR GAME THAT WOULD GENERATE THE EXCITEMENT OF FOOTBALL AND BASEBALL WITHOUT RESULTING IN BROKEN BONES CAUSED BY THE CONFINES OF THE SURROUNDINGS. THE CANADIAN ANSWER: BASKETBALL. INVENTED BY ONTARIO NATIVE JAMES NAISMITH IN 1891, BASKETBALL HAS EVOLVED INTO POSSIBLY THE MOST WIDELY ACCESSIBLE PARTICIPATORY SPORT IN THE WORLD, PLAYED BY KIDS IN OLD SNEAKERS, PEOPLE IN WHEELCHAIRS, MALES AND FEMALES, AMATEURS AND PROFESSIONALS ALIKE. MORE THAN 700,000 CANADIANS OVER THE AGE OF 15 ARE INVOLVED IN SOME FORM OF ORGANIZED BASKETBALL AND ITS POPULARITY AROUND THE CITY OF TORONTO IS INCONTESTABLE — JUST SNEAK A PEEK INTO THE TENS OF THOUSANDS OF CITY DRIVEWAYS WHERE KIDS EVERY DAY LAUNCH BALLS THROUGH HOOPS FOR THE SHEER JOY OF DOING IT.

Appropriately, the very first National Basketball Association game was played in Toronto. The year was 1946 and the New York Knicks squeaked by the hometown Huskies 68-66. Fifty years later to the day, New York returned to celebrate the NBA's half century with their inaugural adversary. This time the Toronto Raptors were on hand to face them, the first non-American team to join the league since the demise of the Huskies 49 years earlier following their fated first – and only – season. The Raptors, however, had gotten off to a more auspicious start, beating the New Jersey Nets in their first game in 1995, the first match in modern history to involve an NBA franchise from outside the U.S.

Raptors fever struck Toronto early and emphatically. A whole year prior to their court debut, team merchandise was selling like hot cakes – $20 million worth in one month alone – putting the embryonic franchise seventh in league merchandise sales even before the first "dunk" was "slammed." And Torontonians' faith has not been misplaced as, at the end of the millennium-straddling season, in their new Air Canada Centre home (the team had moved from SkyDome in 1998), the Raptors became only the third team in NBA history to go from winning less than 20 games a season to making the playoffs with a winning record just two years later.

FOOTBALL

It takes one hundred cows to supply the Canadian Football League with enough leather for a year's supply of balls — and you thought they were pigskins! It also takes 12,000 head of cattle to produce one pound of adrenalin. At that rate, there must be the equivalent of one almighty herd of bovine beasts on the field at each and every Toronto Argonauts' game. Yet the Argos were created as a mere afterthought on October 4, 1873 — something for members of the Argonaut Rowing Club to do to keep themselves fit during the off season. However, they won their very first match — against Hamilton — the following Saturday and by 1883 were able to defeat every team in the newly formed Ontario Rugby Football Union to capture the first championship title.

But it was University of Toronto athletes who had played the first documented football game way back in 1861. And it was they who won the first three Grey Cups — the emblem of Canadian professional football superiority since 1909 — even defeating their crosstown rivals, the Argos, in 1911 to complete their hat trick. It was the Argos, however, who ultimately triumphed. It was they who would evolve into the city's professional football team and become the CFL's all time champs, winning more Grey Cups (14) than any other team in Canada.

Throughout the 20th century, Torontonians attested to their great love of football by being the first to utilize the conveniences of modern life, the better to enjoy the sport. In 1930, Toronto's Balmy Beach faced off against Oshawa under the broad beam of floodlighting, a first for eastern Canada. In 1946, the Argos became the first team to travel by air to meet western teams in preseason games. And in 1952, a Toronto television station became the first to carry a Grey Cup game live when the Canadian Broadcasting Corporation paid $7500 for the privilege of showing the Argos capturing the trophy. The city was also the venue for the first Grey Cup game to be telecast from coast to coast — the year was 1957, and this time television rights sold for the hefty sum of $125,000. Today, those same rights fetch millions.

More than any other city, Toronto is home to the Grey Cup. Local teams have captured the coveted trophy 21 times in its 92-year lifespan, including seven times by University of Toronto, Balmy Beach, and the Toronto RCAF teams. The city has also hosted the championship more often than any other and today is proud to welcome fans to the Argonauts' new home, the ultramodern SkyDome, where eight miles (12.8 km) of zippers hold together a gleaming field of performance-boosting astroturf. Honestly!

A game underway in the old Hanlan's Point Stadium, now the site of the Toronto Island Airport.

A setting sun bathes the SkyDome and CN Tower in golden light as, inside, the Dome's lights have come on to illuminate the Toronto Blue Jays doing battle with a visiting team. Photo: Rick Radell

BASEBALL

Q: The first ever recorded game of "America's national pastime" was played in 1838 in... ? A: Canada! Q: The nationality of the man who handed Babe Ruth his first baseball bat was...? A: Canadian! Yes, Canada has played a significant role in the development of "America's national pastime," often stepping up to the plate and delivering the crucial run. Indeed, the first chapter of what is arguably baseball's most glorious legend was written in... Toronto.

On Saturday, September 5, 1914, at Toronto's 10,000-seat Hanlan's Point Stadium, 19-year-old George Herman "Babe" Ruth was pitching for the Providence Grays against the hometown Maple Leafs in the first half of an International Baseball League double-header. Not only did he pitch a shutout, but he also slammed the first homerun of his long and illustrious professional career with the ball sailing out of the park into the waters of Toronto Bay. In spite of their loss that day, Torontonians are proud to own this piece of baseball history.

Fans leaving the old Maple Leaf Stadium in 1946. Judging by the smiles, we would have to speculate that the Maple Leafs were victorious this day.

Organized ball was played in the city as early as 1859, when a local newspaper reported that the Canadian Pioneers were practicing at the University Grounds every day at four o'clock. By 1886, American sporting goods giant Albert Spalding was promoting Toronto's team as an excellent prospect for the National League, which he had helped found a decade earlier. Ten years later, the popular team moved from the convenience of its downtown ball park to the stadium at Hanlan's Point on Toronto Island – some say for the "convenience" of the team's owner, Lawrence Solman, who also happened to own a commercial ferry service to the island.

When the city expropriated the ferry service some 30 years later, the Maple Leafs moved to a state-of-the-art-for-1926 mainland waterfront facility, Maple Leaf Stadium, near Fleet Street. That year, they won the Little World Series, and for the next 41 seasons, the Fleet Street Flats were home to many good times – and some very bad ones. When the venerable team folded in 1967, only 802 fans were present to witness the last game and the following year the stadium was demolished. However, that dying whimper was expiated a decade later when the Toronto Blue Jays roared onto the scene as members of an expanded American League. The Jays won their very first game and went on that year to set the record for the most wins – 13 – for a first-year expansion club. Major league baseball had arrived in Toronto with a bang.

A glorious Sunday afternoon ball game in progress under the shadow of the CN Tower. The lean in the tower is due to a fish-eye lens and not a rush of Blue Jays fans crowding to the ball-park side of the tower's observation deck.

Maple Leaf Stadium at the foot of Bathurst Street opened in time for the start of the 1926 International Baseball League season. To the left of centre are the new silos at Canada Malting while in the background is the old stadium at Hanlan's Point on the Island. To the west of Maple Leaf Stadium is the office and factory of Tip Top Tailors.

And the Jays didn't disappoint, setting the all-time American League record for attendance (first team ever to draw more than four million fans in one season) and becoming the first non-American World Series Champions, a feat they performed not just once but back-to-back in 1992 and 1993, with a league strike the following season being the only thing between them and a possible hat trick. The world's most advanced and luxurious ballpark – the 600-million-dollar, 50,600-seat SkyDome – may indeed be a fitting home for the making of such baseball history.

A similar view, today.
Still visible are the Crosse and Blackwell Building at the southeast corner of Bathurst Street and Lake Shore Boulevard, the abandoned silos of the Canada Malting Company just east of the foot of Bathurst Street, and the Tip Top Tailor Building on Lake Shore Boulevard. In the background is the Toronto City Centre Airport that opened in the late 1930s as the Port George VI Island Airport some of which covers the site of the old stadium at Hanlan's Point

HOCKEY

NO SPORTING ARENA WAS MORE POPULAR WITH TORONTO FANS THAN THE HOCKEY ARENA. IN 1918, ENTHUSIASTS WERE APPROPRIATELY REWARDED WHEN THE TORONTO ARENAS — FORERUNNERS OF THE MAPLE LEAFS — MADE HISTORY BY BECOMING THE VERY FIRST NATIONAL HOCKEY LEAGUE TEAM EVER TO CAPTURE THE HOLY GRAIL OF HOCKEY, THE STANLEY CUP. AND THE CITY WAS TO MAKE IT TO THE FINALS TWENTY TIMES OVER THE NEXT FIFTY YEARS, EARNING A TOTAL OF 12 CHAMPIONSHIPS INCLUDING TWO GLORIOUS HAT TRICKS IN THE 1947, 1948, 1949 AND 1962, 1963, 1964 SEASONS.

However, not all Cup victories went smoothly. The Leafs' success in 1947 caused team owner Conn Smythe to squirm with embarrassment. Although they were leading the seven-game playoffs three to two, Smythe, in anticipation of a final match-up back in Montreal, was persuaded to leave the Cup in that city while both teams travelled to Toronto for game six. When the Leafs won game six — and thus the championship — the 32-pound trophy (said to weigh "but a feather" in the arms of those who earn it), the oldest trophy competed for by professional athletes in North America, was nowhere to be seen.

The Gardens under construction in the summer of 1931. Both views are to the east along Carlton Street.

Historic Maple Leaf Gardens with flags flying at half mast in homage to the passing of legendary hockey great, Maurice "Rocket" Richard.

"If I were asked by some stranger to North American culture to show him the most important religious building in Canada, I would take him to Toronto's Maple Leaf Gardens."

William Kilbourn, Historian.

In 1902, some decades before the advent of home radio, the Toronto Street Railway Company agreed to put local fans in the picture as soon as possible by "broadcasting" the results of each playoff game by sounding two long blasts on their powerhouse whistle if the hometown team was triumphant, three if defeated. The tension after the second blast must have been palpable for loyal supporters – and even more so for the gamblers among them. That year, Toronto lost to arch rival Montreal.

The first ever radio broadcast of a hockey game was made in 1923 by Foster Hewitt, a Toronto broadcaster and the original voice of Hockey Night in Canada, from the Mutual Street Arena. Pretty soon, the popularity of the sport demanded the construction of a new, larger location – Maple Leaf Gardens. The fact that money for the building was raised during the Great Depression is testimony to the passion of Torontonians for their team. However, construction costs were minimized by striking a deal with labour unions to provide workers with Gardens' stock in place of 20 per cent of their regular earnings.

Toronto's hometown hockey team – whether in its incarnation as the Wellingtons, the Marlboros, the Blueshirts, the Tecumsehs, the Ontarios, the Shamrocks, the Arenas, the St. Patricks or the Maple Leafs; whether in the Mutual Street Arena, Maple Leaf Gardens or the brand new Air Canada Centre – commanded loyalty throughout the 20th century. And fans are hoping the 21st century will be dominated by their heros.

"He shoots! He scores!"

Foster Hewitt March 22, 1923
This is the most famous quotation in the history of sports in Canada.

This photograph, looking north on Yonge Street from Front, was taken soon after the new Head Office of the Bank of Montreal (left) was completed in 1886. In 1993, this gracious old building became home to the Hockey Hall of Fame.

"The Game", a maquette by Edie Parker that draws thousands of camera-toting hockey fans who pose with the life-like, bronze figures at Front and Yonge Street.

A perfect reuse of an old landmark, The Hockey Hall of Fame, today.

"I was born in this city. I was raised in this city. I went from this city to see nearly all of the world, and this is the place I want to live and die."

Gordon Sinclair
He made this comment after touring a still incomplete Tower in 1975.

CN TOWER

ITS ARCHITECTURAL STYLE SAYS IT ALL: EXHIBITIONIST MODERN. THE CN TOWER LAYS CLAIM TO TOO MANY SUPERLATIVES TO LIST, AMONG THEM — AT 181 STOREYS IN HEIGHT — THE WORLD'S TALLEST FREE STANDING STRUCTURE; THE WORLD'S HIGHEST PUBLIC OBSERVATION DECK; THE WORLD'S HIGHEST — AND LARGEST — REVOLVING RESTAURANT; THE WORLD'S HIGHEST WINE CELLAR (ALSO ACKNOWLEDGED AS OFFERING ONE OF THE WORLD'S MOST OUTSTANDING WINE LISTS); THE WORLD'S HIGHEST GLASS FLOOR; THE WORLD'S LONGEST METAL STAIRCASE; AND TRULY ONE OF THE SEVEN WONDERS OF THE MODERN WORLD, AS CONFIRMED BY THE AMERICAN SOCIETY OF CIVIL ENGINEERS.

Ironically, this towering engineering marvel was created to overcome the problems caused by tall buildings in Toronto. The skyscraper office blocks that began to appear in the 1960s interfered with radio and television transmissions and so the decision was made to solve the problem — "with room to spare" — by erecting a communications tower that was taller than the highest building likely to be constructed in the foreseeable future. Today, this tower gives Torontonians the widest choice of television stations in North America, not to mention microwave transmission of voice, telex, computer data, facsimile, radio, telephone and cable traffic. It wasn't until late in the design process, however, that the architects decided to complement the tower's serious purpose by adding tourist features to the picture. Since its opening in 1976, the CN Tower has become one of the city's favourite attractions, and certainly its most visible. As for its name, many people south of the border mistakenly refer to it as the CNN Tower, but it was of course built by the Canadian National Railway. In 1997,

TrizecHahn Corporation signed a long-term operating and management lease for the Tower and now the CN of CN Tower stands for Canada's National Tower.

Said to have been constructed with enough concrete to pave a sidewalk all the way to Montreal, 460 kilometres (285 miles) to the east, the tower — the first (and only) of its kind — demanded solutions to engineering problems that had never before been addressed. Its highest observation deck is able to sway seven feet from side to side in complete safety during 325 kilometres per hour (200 mph) wind gusts. It is almost farcical that this envelope-pushing project which advanced the state of engineering in our time has been used for such frivolities as demonstrating that an egg dropped from a height of 341.37 metres (1120 feet) can land unscathed. But this only works when it's a Grade 'A' egg. Of course.

The city's skyscrapers stare up at the CN Tower.

Aerial view of the downtown core looking north east over the top of the CN Tower. The tower's dominance of the city skyline seems secure from this lofty vantage point.

Members of "The Audience", Michael Snow's wonderful sculpture at the entrance to SkyDome, seem to be pointing out the CN Tower to passers-by.

The CN Tower climbs ever higher in this fall, 1973 photograph. At the base of the tower is the 1928 CP Roundhouse and in the foreground the John Street water pumping station complex which was moved later to permit SkyDome to be built on the site.

The CN Tower was constructed using the slipform method. Concrete from a batching plant at the base of the tower was continually poured (except for weekends) into the slipform which was jacked higher and higher until the full height of the concrete portion of the tower was reached. Summer, 1973.

ONTARIO PLACE

Ontario Place, today. The Toronto skyline looms in the distance.

WHEN MONTREAL GOT THE NOD AS THE HOST CITY FOR THE **1967** WORLD'S FAIR, TORONTO CITY OFFICIALS AND THEIR PROVINCIAL COUNTERPARTS FELT SOMETHING EXTRA SPECIAL HAD TO BE DONE LOCALLY TO CELEBRATE CANADA'S CENTENNIAL ANNIVERSARY. THE CITY DECIDED TO PUT ADDITIONAL MONEY INTO THAT YEAR'S CANADIAN NATIONAL EXHIBITION, TRANSFORMING THE BANDSHELL INTO A GIANT "CAKE" TOPPED WITH BIRTHDAY "CANDLES" WITH HOME-GROWN TALENT PERFORMING FOR ENTHUSIASTIC AUDIENCES. THE PROVINCE, MEANWHILE, PLANNED A **$5,000,000** BIRTHDAY GIFT FOR ITS CITIZENS. HOWEVER, THAT BIRTHDAY GIFT, THE ONTARIO CENTENNIAL CENTRE OF SCIENCE AND TECHNOLOGY IN SUBURBAN DON MILLS, FAILED TO OPEN AS PLANNED ON CANADA DAY **1967**.

First, a trio of obsolete lake freighters were sunk to prevent the erosion of newly reclaimed land at the Ontario Place site. 1969.

Next, new land is formed using excavated material from various city construction sites. 1970.

On May 22, 1971, Ontario Place was officially opened to the general public. Adult admission was a buck.

Embarrassed that its own centennial project, the Science Centre, was way behind schedule and realizing that the CNE hadn't been able to generate the kind of excitement enjoyed by the hugely successful Montreal Expo '67, the Ontario government announced in the fall of 1968 that it would assist the CNE in creating "a whole new fair." In addition, it would build a state-of-the-art entertainment and leisure complex on three "Expo '67-style" islands to be constructed in Lake Ontario adjoining the CNE Grounds.

While the government had spoken briefly with CNE officials about creating a "whole new fair," this was the first time they had heard about the new waterfront project, which they viewed as being in direct competition with their annual fair. Then the other shoe dropped. When Ontario Place was completed, the province would move out of the CNE's Ontario Government Building where it had put on a display every year since 1926. A double whammy! Regardless, the new islands quickly began to emerge from the lake in March 1969 as huge fleets of trucks dumped massive quantities of material from construction

sites around the city including the new Commerce Court skyscraper downtown and excavation of the Yonge Street subway extension north of Eglinton. Within days, City Council was crying foul about the lack of consultation. Provincial officials retaliated by claiming title to all the land under Lake Ontario. And this unhappy inter-government animosity continued for many months.

To protect the new islands from an often turbulent lake, a trio of freighters – the *Howard L. Shaw, the Victorious* and the *Douglas Houghton* – was towed to the site, sunk and positioned to form an impenetrable breakwater. Today, these freighters also protect a public marina with docking for 300 vessels, allowing countless visitors every year to berth just minutes from downtown Toronto and mere steps from the many attractions of Ontario Place (including what was the world's first permanent Imax™ theatre). Indeed – in spite of those early fears – these same visitors are also just a stone's throw from the continuing late summer allure of the CNE.

CANADIAN NATIONAL EXHIBITION

THE WILL TO SURVIVE AGAINST THE ODDS HAS MADE THE CANADIAN NATIONAL EXHIBITION A WINNER AMONGST COMMUNITY FAIRS. WAY BACK IN 1879, THE PROVINCIAL AGRICULTURAL ASSOCIATION, THE BODY RESPONSIBLE FOR SELECTING THE LOCATION OF THE YEARLY PROVINCIAL FAIR, REFUSED TORONTO'S REQUEST TO HOST THE EVENT ON AN ANNUAL BASIS AND THE CITY FATHERS, ANGERED BUT UNDAUNTED, REBELLED. AFTER ALL, HADN'T THE PREVIOUS YEAR'S FAIR, WHICH THEY HAD HOSTED, BEEN AN UNQUALIFIED SUCCESS? WHAT MORE EVIDENCE DID GOVERNMENT OFFICIALS NEED TO CONVINCE THEM TO HOLD ALL FUTURE FAIRS IN THE PROVINCIAL CAPITAL? SO WHEN THE 1879 FAIR WAS AWARDED TO THE CITY OF OTTAWA, THE TORONTO PROMOTERS, UNDER THE LEADERSHIP OF ALDERMAN JOHN J. WITHROW, VOWED TO ORGANIZE THEIR OWN.

The Princes' Gates under construction, 1927. Originally built as the Diamond Jubilee of Confederation Gates (to celebrate the 60th anniversary of Canadian confederation) the fact that Edward, the Prince of Wales and George, the Duke of Kent were present to officially dedicate the structure resulted in the less effusive term Princes' Gates.

The Princes' Gates, a CNE landmark since 1927.

CNE poster for the 1927 fair featuring the new Princes' Gates.

The CNE Grandstand (left) and the mammoth Dance Tent (bottom) are but two features in this late 1940s aerial view of the CNE.

The double ferris wheels are packed in this 1940s view of the midway.

And what a fair they created, determined to make it grander in every way than anything put together by the agricultural board. It even had a more imposing title – the Toronto Industrial Exhibition – to indicate that, rather than limiting itself to displays of purely agricultural interest, this fair would be a national showplace (the name was later changed to the Canadian National Exhibition) where the latest wonders from the world of industry and technology would also be on display. That list of wonders would, over time, include the telephone, the phonograph, a streetcar that received its power from an overhead wire, automobiles, wireless radios, stoves, refrigerators and so much more. Many of these items were first seen by Canadians at the CNE.

Once the only summer game in town, the "Grand Old Lady of the Waterfront" still attracts nearly a million-and-a-half visitors during its 18-day run each summer, still showcasing the latest in technology as well as agricultural displays and diverse family entertainment – and still beating the odds, this time against 21st century air conditioned mercantile temples, interactive theme parks and the simple comfort of sitting at home in front of a 40-inch television set, a technology that was first introduced to amazed fair-goers at the 1938 edition of the CNE.

Portion of the midway in the 1940s when candy apples could be had for a nickel.

An "all ladies orchestra" serenaded visitors to an early Automobile Show held in the CNE's Transportation Building. c1920.

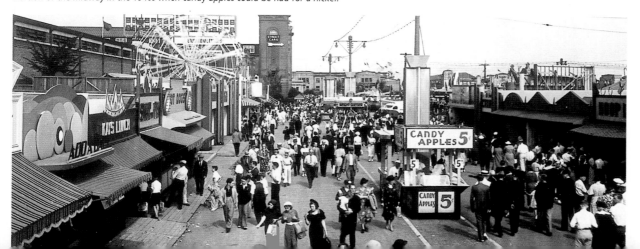

"WILD RACES OF AUTOS" screamed the headline of August 6th, 1903. *"Exciting Event Was Automobile Races at Exhibition Park - Mile a Minute Almost Reached."* The article began; *"A royal spectacle was the automobile races at Exhibition Park on Saturday. The big cars careening around the track, their powerful engines puffing and snorting, keyed the nerves of the spectators to the highest pitch of excitement".*

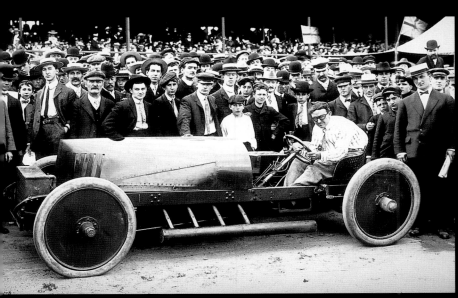

Barney Oldfield posing in his "Peerless" 100 horse power racer prior to an attempt to beat his own world record

Aerial view of the Molson Indy race as the cars pass the Princes' Gate and hit the long straight-away

AIRPORTS

TORONTO'S FIRST AIRPORT WASN'T AN AIRPORT AT ALL. IT WAS, IN FACT, A 243-HECTARE (600-ACRE) WORKING FARM LOCATED SEVERAL MILES NORTHWEST OF THE CITY, NOT FAR FROM THE LITTLE COMMUNITY OF WESTON IN THE RURAL TOWNSHIP OF YORK. THE DECISION TO USE THE FARM AS AN AIRFIELD WAS MADE BY THE ORGANIZING COMMITTEE RESPONSIBLE FOR A SERIES OF PIONEER FLYING MEETS PLANNED FOR VARIOUS LOCATIONS ACROSS CANADA. AMONG THE PARTICIPANTS ATTENDING THE TORONTO MEET WAS FRENCH AVIATOR JACQUES DE LESSEPS, SON OF COUNT FERDINAND DE LESSEPS, BUILDER OF THE SUEZ CANAL. ON JULY 13, 1910, THE YOUNG DE LESSEPS TOOK OFF FROM THE YORK TOWNSHIP PASTURE AND FLEW HIS BLERIOT NO. 9 BIPLANE SOUTHEASTERLY. IN DOING SO, HE BECAME THE FIRST PERSON TO FLY A HEAVIER-THAN-AIR MACHINE OVER THE CITY. AND IT SHOULD BE REMEMBERED THAT THIS FEAT TOOK PLACE JUST SEVEN YEARS AFTER THE WRIGHT BROTHERS' FIRST HEAVIER-THAN-AIR MACHINE TOOK TO THE AIR OVER KITTYHAWK, NORTH CAROLINA AND ONLY A LITTLE MORE THAN A YEAR AFTER J.A.D. MCCURDY'S FIRST FLIGHT IN CANADA ON FEBRUARY 23RD, 1909.

Several years later, as aviation began to interest people not only as a sport but also as a business, that Weston farm meadow became a real airfield and was given the name de Lesseps Field. Other airfields appeared in suburban Long Branch and on the sandbar at the west end of Toronto Island. Then, with the advent of the Great War, airplanes suddenly became military tools and two more airfields were needed for pilot training – Leaside Aerodrome on Eglinton Avenue East near Laird, and Armour Heights, not far from the present Avenue Road-Highway 401 interchange. It was here in 1917 that a young Amelia Earhart, working as a nurse's aide at the nearby Spadina Military Hospital, began to consider flying as a career.

J.A.D. McCurdy, of Silver Dart fame at the controls of an early Curtis pusher biplane in 1911.

Canadian Airlines Boeing 747 flight deck reflects a half century of cockpit evolution.

Aerial view of Toronto City Centre Airport showing just how conveniently it is situated adjacent to the downtown core of the city.

Malton Airport looking north along Airport Road in 1939.

Renamed Toronto International Airport in 1960, the new "Aeroquay" (Terminal 1) was opened in 1964 by then Prime Minister Lester Pearson. The airposrt was renamed in his honour in 1984.

Toronto Island Airport in the late 1930s.

Aerial view of Malton Airport 1953.

With the return of peace, aviation took off. Commercial fields sprang up all across the city, one on north Yonge Street in Willowdale, another on the west side of Dufferin Street north of Lawrence, and two additional fields near the present Dufferin and Wilson intersection. In 1929, a harbour for seaplanes was added to the waterfront at the foot of Yonge Street. But all of these facilities were primitive in nature, most with grass landing strips and all with few amenities, until the de Havilland Aircraft Company Airport entered the scene in 1929 in suburban Downsview. There, many successful aircraft were conceived, built and first took to the air – aircraft with names like Chipmunk, the Twin Otter and, more recently, the Dash-7, the Dash-8, and the Global Express. The airport also served for some decades as an active Royal Canadian Air Force/Canadian Armed Forces airfield and was the location in 1946 of the very first edition of the Canadian International Air Show.

However, until 1938, Toronto's primitive commercial airfields were frequently the butt of jokes by aviators from around the world. Then, thanks to the efforts of World War I flying ace and former Toronto mayor Bert Wemp and Toronto booster and future mayor Allan Lamport, the city made the decision to build not one but two modern airfields. The main one was situated on reclaimed land at the west end of Toronto Island and was named Port George VI Island Airport to mark the first visit to the city by a reigning monarch in 1939. Interestingly, the first commercial flight to land here carried Tommy Dorsey and his Orchestra. The boys had come to town to entertain at that summer's Canadian National Exhibition. Today, the airport has been renamed Toronto City Centre, a marketing strategy to emphasize its proximity to the downtown core.

Entrance to Malton Airport, 1940s.

Construction of a new terminal is underway, with the soon to be demolished Terminals 1 and 2 in the background.

Terminal 3, newest of the three operating facilities, today.

The second airfield was simply to be a backup emergency landing field and was constructed on flat lands near the village of Malton, some miles to the northwest of the city. When Malton Airport opened in September 1938, its first terminal was in the old Chapman farmhouse near the Sixth Line, now Airport Road. The following year, a 35 metres by 11.5 metres (116 feet by 38 feet) terminal was constructed, complete with a control tower – but no air traffic controllers. Malton went on to spawn the C-102 – the first jetliner to fly in North America – and the CF-105 Avro Arrow twin engine supersonic interceptor, both developed by Malton's Avro Aircraft Company. When the Arrow was abruptly and bafflingly cancelled in 1959, many of its designers were snatched up by the fledgling NASA space program.

Today, the airport on Toronto Island airport serves mainly pleasure and small corporate aircraft plus some inter-city propeller-driven flights, and Malton Airport – renamed Toronto International in 1960 and Pearson International in 1984 – is now Canada's largest and busiest air terminus handling more than 14 million passengers and nearly 200 million tons of cargo each year. No one is laughing at the city's aviation record now.

Dixon Side Road looking west past Highway 27 towards Malton Airport, still operating in its very rural setting in 1959. Promoters' billboards proclaim the glories of their forthcoming luxury hotels.

HOTEL STRIP

When it was first announced that one of Toronto's two new airports was to be located near the tiny rural community of Malton the news was met with great derision. Many regarded the location as being too far out in the country and as a result air travellers would never use it. Some experts suggested that a better site for the new airport was near the corner of Dufferin Street and Wilson Avenue in North York Township.

Dixon Road looking west, today. Hotels now crowd all four corners at the Carlingview Road intersection. In the distance is the Highway 427 overpass and further still the sprawling Lester B. Pearson International Airport.

CANADA'S first *Cloverleaf* Intersection

The handling of constantly increasing traffic on Canada's busiest roadways is only partially solved by Dual Highways. Delays at important intersections can be best prevented by avoiding all left-hand turns. The Cloverleaf at Cooksville, Ont., on the new Middle Road between Toronto and Hamilton is a practical solution to the problem of speeding up traffic safely. It is built of concrete for permanence and low maintenance cost.

CANADA CEMENT COMPANY LIMITED
Office — 803 Northern Ontario Building — Toronto

Newspaper advertisement placed by the Canada Cement Company, Limited explaining the virtues of the highway cloverleaf and why it should be built out of concrete, 1937.

Queen Elizabeth Highway and Highway 10 interchange looking to the north east.

CLOVERLEAF

One of the most interesting features of the new Queen Elizabeth Highway was the incorporation of a "cloverleaf" at the point where it met Highway 10 just north of Port Credit. Constructed in 1937, this was the first use of this now commonplace highway feature. At first, drivers were confused, having to turn right to go left. To help out, plenty of explanatory signs were posted and extra police assigned to the intersection in an effort to assist drivers with the unfamiliar manoeuvres.

Queen Elizabeth Highway looking east, c1940.

Queen Elizabeth Highway looking west over the Dixie interchange today and c.1936.

QEW AT DIXIE ROAD

The thought of another world war was far from people's minds as they cheered King George VI and Queen Elizabeth when the royal couple officially dedicated the new Queen Elizabeth Way at the Henley Bridge near St. Catharines in 1939. The new highway was built in response to ever-increasing traffic volumes on the existing Dundas Highway and Lakeshore Road. The Toronto-Hamilton stretch of the new highway followed the old Middle Road (whose location between the two older highways was the reason for its name) and in doing so caused little controversy amongst property owners. The Hamilton-Niagara Falls section, on the other hand, ripped through hundreds of acres of fertile farm fields. These property owners were highly critical of the government's actions and in several cases compared the acquisition of their properties to "Herr Hitler's tactics in Europe."

The first part of the new QEW to open was the four-lane connection between Niagara Falls and Highway 27 on Toronto's western outskirts and was touted as having the longest continuous lighting system in the world. One year later, in the summer of 1940, the Highway 27 to the Humber River section opened. Another year passed before the Niagara Falls to Fort Erie stretch was passable although it remained gravel-surfaced until paving could be completed in 1956.

Rush hour on Yonge Street in 1929.

Aerial view of interchange at 401 and Don Valley Parkway looking to the north east.

DON VALLEY PARKWAY

The idea of using the valley of the lower Don River as the location for a highway to ease the city's ever increasing north-south traffic congestion was first suggested as early as 1931 at a cost of $1.6 million. Starting at the mouth of the Don, the proposed highway would follow the east bank of the river to just north of the Bloor-Danforth Viaduct where it would branch into three; one route connecting with Mount Pleasant Road at Merton Street, another with Moore Avenue near Bayview and a third continuing north and east to Woodbine Avenue near O'Connor Drive. In an effort to kickstart the project – touted as an answer for the thousands of Torontonians out of work due to the Great Depression – several landowners in the valley even offered to donate portions of their property. However, it was not approved by the electorate until 1947 and it would take another 11 years for any actual work to begin, plus another eight to reach completion. Its route altered so that it connected the recently completed Gardiner Expressway (that traversed Toronto's waterfront) with the new Highway 401 (that stretched across the city's northern limits), the $40 million DVP highway finally opened to traffic in 1966.

Construction of Don Valley Parkway in the late 1950s.

Rush hour on the Don Valley Parkway south of Lawrence.

View looking north over the Gerrard Street Bridge towards the Prince Edward Viaduct that carries Bloor Street across the Don Valley, c.1950. The Don Jail and Riverdale Hospital appear at centre right. Note in the contemporary photo that the old warehouse at bottom left has been converted to a parking garage for the apartment complex that appeared in the half century seperating these two images.

The Riverdale Hospital, close to the banks of the Don, can trace its roots back to the "House of Refuge" which opened its doors to small pox victims in 1860. Later, in the 20th century, renamed the Riverdale Isolation Hospital, it continued to treat the odd case of small pox along with the dreaded polio and scarlet fever. Today the facility specializes in chronic care.

The nearby Don Jail, actually the fourth jail for the city, was opened in 1864 and continued to house prisoners until the end of 1977. The new section, built in 1958, continues to operate today, although there are plans to close it in the next few years. Toronto's first jail was a small wooden structure occupying the site of today's King Edward Hotel on King Street.

"The Don River used to run through the Don Valley, which was once one of the most beautiful valleys in all of southern Ontario. Now the Don Valley Parkway runs through the Don Valley and the Don River hardly runs at all."

Arthur Black
Broadcaster and humourist.

Don Valley Parkway looking north over the Gerrard Street Bridge towards the Prince Edward Viaduct. The expanded Don Jail and Riverdale Hospital are visible at centre right.

Contemporary aerial view looking south over the Eglinton Avenue interchange at the Don Valley Parkway.

For dramatic changes in a relatively short, 50 year period, it would be difficult to find a better example than the area of the Don Valley Parkway between Lawrence and Eglinton.

The large photo at left is an aerial view to the south over the Eglinton Avenue interchange. Note the rail line angling to the south at left center and the V-shaped Crowne Plaza Hotel visible at bottom left. Now see if you can find the same railway in the small photo below taken in 1958. You will see Eglinton Avenue running across the bottom of the photo and the horse barn and corrals of the old Fleming farm at bottom right are now occupied by the hotel visible in the contemporary aerial view on the opposite page.

Similarly, the rail line will provide the connecting elements in the two photos to the right. The old wooden bridge visible in the 1949 black and white photo, carries a narrow dirt path called Lawrence Avenue over the tracks of the Canadian National Railway. This line is now used by GO Transit's commuter trains on the Richmond Hill route.

Contemporary aerial view to the north over the Lawrence Avenue interchange on the Don Valley Parkway.

View south over Eglinton Avenue and the Don River, 1949.

View north over Lawrence Avenue, 1958.

Aerial view looking north on the new Highway 400 under construction at its interchange with old Highway 7, c.1950.

HIGHWAY 400

In the fall of 1944 officials of the Ontario government announced plans to construct a 96 kilometre (60 mile) long "super highway" that would connect Toronto and Barrie. But, as a result of problems associated with acquiring property and shortages of cement and steel (what little there was had been re-directed for use in the construction of electric power stations) the highway wasn't opened until 1951. This despite the fact that the section from the Maple Side Road (now Major Mackenzie Drive) to Barrie would not be paved until the following year.

Contemporary view looking north on Highway 400 at the interchanges with the new Highway 407 (foreground) and Highway 7.

HIGHWAY 401

Opened in late 1947, a new four-lane highway known as Highway 2A connected Scarborough with the City of Oshawa 30 kilometres (18 miles) to the east. This stretch of modern highway was to be the genesis of today's Macdonald-Cartier Freeway.

Over the next few years traffic throughout the Toronto area grew dramatically and soon engineers were looking for a way to divert traffic around the city. Eventually the provincial government began purchasing farm land in North York Township for a 300-foot wide right-of-way. Many transportation critics thought that a traffic corridor so far north of the city was absolute folly and called the whole exercise a monumental waste of the taxpayers' hard earned money. Despite all the critics by late 1952 a new, four-lane, 12 kilometre (7 mile), limited access highway between Weston Road and Yonge Street called, naturally enough, the Toronto Bypass was open to traffic.

Looking east on Highway 401 at the interchanges with Highway 400.

Aerial view looking east on Highway 401 over the Highway 400 interchange as construction appears to be nearing completion, 1953.

By 1955, the highway had been extended east to Bayview Avenue and, five months later, west to Highway 27. In late summer 1956, the Toronto Bypass finally attained the engineers' original goal when it was lengthened an additional 19 kilometres (12 miles) to connect with Scarborough's Highway 2A. At last, some 48,000 vehicles a day could travel the 38 kilometres (24 miles) across Toronto without causing chaos on city streets. In the years that followed, Highway 401 was being used by more and more drivers as a shortcut between places within the city and not for the through-traffic purposes for which it was originally planned. Taking a cue from Chicago where the same problem had arisen, in 1962 a project to widen the highway from four to 12 (16 in some places) lanes got underway. The idea was to place "through" traffic in centre "express lanes" with all other traffic confined to outer "collector lanes." Access between these categories was kept to a minimum in order to encourage drivers setting out on lengthy trips to use the centre lanes only.

Today, Highway 401/Macdonald-Cartier Freeway (the latter title selected in 1965 by Ontario Premier John Robarts to honour two of Canada's "Fathers of Confederation," Sir John A. Macdonald and Sir Georges-Étienne Cartier) is 820 kilometres (510 miles) in length. It has a rush hour peak of nearly 380,000 vehicles per day through the Toronto area, making it the second busiest highway on the North American continent.

*They are too near
To be great
But our children
Shall understand
When and how our
Fate was changed
And by whose hand.*

Rudyard Kipling 1917

THE GREAT WAR

OF THE **400** IMAGES IN THIS BOOK, THIS IS THE ONE I AM CONTINUALLY DRAWN BACK TO. THE ARCHIVAL CAPTION TELLS US VERY LITTLE: "VISITOR'S DAY AT THE CNE, 1915". BUT LOOK AT THE FACES. THE BABY, UNAWARE, UNAFRAID, INTRIGUED BY ALL NEW THINGS SHE HAS BEEN EXPOSED TO DURING THIS DAY. THE TWO YOUNG SOLDIERS SOON TO BOARD THE TRAIN AT THE OLD UNION STATION FOR THE TRENCHES OF EUROPE. TO SURVIVE THERE FOR MORE THAN TWO BLOODY YEARS - WHAT ARE THEIR CHANCES? WOULD THEY FIGHT AT VIMY RIDGE? IF SO, WOULD THEY SURVIVE THIS DEFINING MOMENT OF THEIR YOUNG COUNTRY OR WOULD THEY BE AMONG THE MORE THAN **60,000** CANADIAN SOLDIERS WHO WOULD NOT COME HOME? ARE THEY FRIENDS FROM THE SAME TOWN, BROTHERS PERHAPS, OR DID THEY MEET AND BECOME PART OF SHAKESPEARE'S 'BAND OF BROTHERS' DURING THEIR PREPARATION FOR WAR - ON THE GROUNDS OF THE CANADIAN NATIONAL EXHIBITION? AND THE WOMAN! FEAR AND UNCERTAINTY IN THE EYES AS EVENTS ON THE FAR-AWAY WORLD STAGE OVERWHELM HER? HER HUSBAND OFF TO AN UNCERTAIN FUTURE! A NEW BABY IN ARMS. HOW MUCH DID SHE - DID ANYONE THERE THAT DAY - KNOW OF WHAT LAY AHEAD? ARE ANY OF THEM HIDDEN SOMEWHERE IN THE TWO PHOTOS OPPOSITE, TAKEN THREE YEARS APART? HOW DID THEIR LIVES EVOLVE AFTER THIS TINY FRAGMENT OF TIME BURNED ITSELF ONTO A PIECE OF FILM?

JOHN MCQUARRIE

Crowds gather to wish the boys of the 180th Battalion 'good luck' as the next troop train leaves Toronto's old Union Station west of York Street.

No sooner had Great Britain declared war on Germany in the summer of 1914, than Canada (and the rest of the British Empire) was at war too. In Toronto, officials originally thought that the upcoming annual Exhibition should be cancelled. Seeing the potential of using the fair as a giant recruiting centre it was decided that the Ex would go on as usual. Part of the grounds became a military camp and when the Ex was in progress, various bands would parade through the grounds. Guns and planes and other war equipment were put on display. For the young male visitors to the fair, it was just too good to pass up.

"For King and Country!!", was the cry.

"Where do I sign up", came the reply.

Many young Torontonians answered the call. Ten thousand did not come home.

Torontonians went wild on Armistice Day, November 11, 1918. Streetcars try to navigate through the jubilant crowds at the packed King and Yonge intersection.

The Great Western Railway station, southeast corner of Yonge and Front streets, c1880.

Canadian Pacific Railway's new North Toronto Station soon after it opened in 1916.

The former CPR North Toronto Station in its present incarnation as a liquor store at the corner of Yonge and Scrvener.

South facade of the old Union Station c.1880. Buildings visible in right background are on Front Street West..

TORONTO AND IT'S TRAINS

IN THE SPRING OF 1853, MORE THAN THIRTY YEARS BEFORE TRANS-CONTINENTAL RAILWAY WOULD BE COMPLETED ACROSS CANADA, CROWDS CHEERED AND ELECTED OFFICIALS BEAMED WITH PRIDE AS THE PROVINCE'S FIRST STEAM TRAIN CHUGGED OUT OF THE LITTLE WOODEN STATION ON THE SOUTH SIDE OF TORONTO'S FRONT STREET AND INTO THE HISTORY BOOKS.

The O.S.&H., or more formally, the Ontario, Simcoe and Huron Railway (a title that identified the trio of Great Lakes that the company would serve) had many detractors, still not convinced that these new-fangled steam railways were worth the expense. They mockingly referred to the new project as the Oats, Straw and Hay.

Skepticism of the day made financing railways difficult. And when the new line's pioneer promoter and first manager, Frederick Capreol, suggested raising money by selling thousands of Grand Canadian Railroad Lottery tickets, the prizes to consist of $2 million worth of land and stocks, he was quickly dubbed "Mad Capreol". Those opposed to his plan charged that a lottery fed on "a strong temptation to attain wealth without labour" and that anyone promoting such a "demoralizing device" must have private gain in mind. Contrary to today's wide use of lotteries as fund-raisers, the mid-19th century belief that they were the work of the devil made them unsavoury. More conventional methods of financing eventually won the day and, after months of hard work, Capreol's dream started to take shape with the obligatory sod-turning ceremony on October 15, 1851. Unfortunately, Capreol was not present. His "immoral" lottery scheme had not been forgotten and he was fired just two days before the first sod was turned.

UNION STATION

Even though Edward, the Prince of Wales had officially opened the magnificent new structure with the requisite pomp and ceremony in the summer of 1927, railway travellers were still unable to use the new facility. The reason is apparent in the aerial view (below), the tracks are still well to the south of the new station. This situation would continue to exist for another decade.

The location of the railway tracks relative to the city's new railway station had been an ongoing problem virtually since the day officials decided that a new station would, in fact, be built. Unable to decide upon a location for the massive new viaduct that would be acceptable to all the participants meant that the new station would be ready long before the trains could access it. In fact, the final positioning of the viaduct on which the tracks would be located dragged on years after the interior of the station was complete. This resulted in customers being forced to continue to use the old station even though the new one appeared to be ready. Then, once the old station had been demolished, customers were inconvenienced further by having to make their way through the new station's Great Hall to the trains that were waiting at the old station's platforms. The situation was untenable and resulted in a plethora of scathing newspaper editorials. More than three years would pass before the new viaduct and railway concourse would finally be completed and the tracks redirected into the new station.

"Hurry up and wait" seemed to be the motto of Toronto's new Union Station. More than a quarter-of-a-century had gone by since that day in 1905 when federal government officials ordered that a new Union Station be built to serve Toronto's railway travelling public and the day the trains began using the marvellous new station on a regular basis.

Union Station nearing completion, 1918.

Union Station, 1920. Ready for everything but trains.

Union Station, 1928. Old Union Station is at the extreme left of the photograph as is a portion of the former York Street "temporary" bridge. To the right is Bay Street with a leg of the Bay Street running off to the right of the view. The Bay street cars used this bridge to circumvent the dangerous level crossing on Bay south of Front. The present Bay Street underpass opened a year after this picture was taken. Union Station

173

HOTELS AND THE RAILWAY

Railways and hotels have long enjoyed a symbiotic relationship and nowhere is this more evident than in the Canadian Pacific Railway's century-old tradition of building magnificent hotels along its main line from coast to coast. Their "chateau style" has become the one uniquely Canadian architectural statement. Apart from Toronto's grand old Royal York, prime examples include the Banff Springs, Empress, Chateau Lake Louise, Chateau Laurier, Palizer and Queen Elizabeth.

In these three photographs we see Union Station's busy exterior, elegant interior, the old clock and Francesco Pirelli's bronze sculpture called 'Monument to Multiculturalism.

View east along Front Street, 1925. Union Station is visible on the right and the Queen's Hotel occupies the future site of the Royal York Hotel. In the photo below the Queen's is gone and work on the excavation for the Royal York is well underway.

Aerial view of the Royal York looking northeast over Union Station.

View of the Royal York looking west along Front Street.

In this wonderful old photo, c.1928, finishing touches are being applied to both the Royal York Hotel and Union Station.

TORONTO TRANSIT COMMISSION

THE IMPLEMENTATION OF CERTAIN PUBLIC AMENITIES SUCH AS SIDEWALKS AND SEWERS WAS HIGH ON THE LIST OF "THINGS TO DO" WHEN TORONTO WAS INCORPORATED IN 1834, BUT PUBLIC TRANSPORTATION WAS NOT AMONG THEM. IN FACT, ANOTHER 15 YEARS WOULD GO BY BEFORE ANYONE THOUGHT ABOUT OFFERING SUCH A SERVICE. IT WAS IN 1849 THAT A YONGE STREET CABINET MAKER AND OCCASIONAL UNDERTAKER, HENRY BURT WILLIAMS, INTRODUCED A FLEET OF FOUR SIX-PASSENGER BUSES THAT RAN BETWEEN THE ST. LAWRENCE MARKET AND THE RED LION INN ON THE EAST SIDE OF YONGE STREET, A FEW BLOCKS NORTH OF THE BLOOR STREET CROSSING. WHAT GAVE MR. BURT'S OPERATION PARTICULAR APPEAL WAS THE NOVEL CONCEPT THAT HIS CONVEYANCES FOLLOWED A PRINTED TIMETABLE. PASSENGERS KNEW WHEN BUSES WOULD LEAVE EACH TERMINAL, THE TIME BETWEEN BUSES, AND JUST HOW LONG IT WOULD TAKE TO GET FROM POINT A TO POINT B. AND WHILE INCLEMENT WEATHER MIGHT SLOW THINGS DOWN, NEVERTHELESS IT WAS A SURE BET THAT THE BUSES WOULD STILL OPERATE — NOT A COMMON EXPERIENCE IN THOSE DAYS.

When a heavy snowfall clogged Toronto streetcar lines in 1891, the transportation company's new "twelve horsepower" sweeper made short work of the clean-up. In this photo the vehicle is being used to transport dignitaries to the cornerstone laying ceremonies at what is now old City Hall.

The Toronto Railway Company's open electric streetcar 375 had already seen ten years of service when this photo was taken at at Dovercourt Road and Van Horne Avenue (now Dupont Street) in 1904.

Henry Burt Williams' ten-passenger omnibus in front of the Red Lion Inn, east side of Yonge Street north of Bloor, typical of the public transit vehicles operating in 1850.

Streetcars, like this pair near the intersection of King and Simcoe, still rule the downtown today.

Commuters leaving streetcar at the corner of Queen and Bay, 1905.

In 1861, following the incorporation of the Toronto Street Railway (TSR), tracks were laid on Yonge Street and horse-drawn streetcars were introduced. These conveyances became extremely popular and quickly put poor Mr. Burt out of business. The surviving enterprise was soon in a position to build additional lines and before long the city could claim that it offered a respectable public transit system. Horses gave way to horsepower of a different kind when the successor to the TSR, the Toronto Railway Company (TRC), introduced the first of its electric streetcars in 1892. The last horse plodded down McCaul Street two years later.

The TRC would go on to hold a 30-year monopoly over the city's transit system, making its backers happy but frustrating people who lived in areas outside the busy core when the company refused to extend its tracks into places where passenger traffic was minimal. A legal battle ensued. The TRC's position was upheld by the highest courts but the rift that had developed between the city and the company ultimately led to the establishment of a municipally-controlled public transit authority.

The new Toronto Transportation Commission (now the Toronto Transit Commission) took over operations on September 1, 1921. Today, the TTC operates a fleet of 1483 buses, 660 subway cars, 250 streetcars and 28 Intermediate Capacity Transit System vehicles. They cover 147 routes over some 6500 kilometres (4000 miles). With an average daily ridership of nearly 1.3 million, the TTC has the highest per capita ridership on the North American continent. It is second only to New York City in the percentage of downtown workers who use public transit to commute in the morning rush hour period. In addition, since 1973, the American Public Transit Association has named the TTC the safest transit system in the world more than 20 times.

Toronto Railway Company trainmen pose for the photographer in front of the old Roncesvalles car house, 1907.

In 1923, crews of the two-year-old Toronto Transportation Commission rebuilt the King, Queen, Roncesvalles, Queensway, Lake Shore intersection, one of the most complicated on the continent, in less than 24 hours. This view looks northwest from King Street.

Operators in front of the "new" (1923) Roncesvalles car house. "Roncy" has been an operating streetcar division since 1895.

Similar view of same intersection today.

One of the TTC's large Peter Witt streetcars in front of Union Station, 1932.

Yonge Street, just north of Queen, is being ripped up as crews build the the first of the city's new subway lines, 1950. The 12 station Yonge Street line ran from Union Station to Eglinton Avenue. Opened in 1954, the fare was 3 tickets/tokens for a quarter or ten cents cash. The idea of building what was originally called a "tube line" was first put forward in 1910 and while the concept was approved by the electorate nothing happened until the ceremonial first pile was driven at the corner of Yonge and Wellington streets in the fall of 1949.

Today, the TTC operates two subway routes, the 30.2 kilometre (18.8 mile) Yonge, University, Spadina line and the 26.2 kilometre (16.3 mile) Bloor-Danforth line. More than 830,000 people use the rapid transit system each weekday. Pictured above is the ultra-modern Downsview subway station. This most recent subway extension took place in the Spring of 1996.

Yonge Street looking north at the future site of the Davisville Shops and the new TTC head office building, 1951.

Yonge Street looking north to Eglinton Avenue, 1951. The Eglinton streetcar barn is now the site of a mammoth office building that incorporates the Eglinton subway station.

Yonge Street looking north to Eglinton Avenue today. Note how the presence of a subway station has attracted a huge proliferation of apartment buildings and condominium towers. Many of these towers have direct, underground tunnels leading to the subway station, allowing residents to travel to and from many of the downtown office towers without ever venturing outside. This can mean heavy winter clothing stays at home until the weekend.

WINTER

Toronto used to have winter - the sort of winter artists who live in California paint on Christmas cards. But, be it global warming or the whims of our planet's weather Gods, our climate is growing more temperate. Torontonians with a number higher than '4' in front of their birthdays can remember a time when the harbour used to freeze solid. You could actually skate to the Island if you were so inclined. Kids loved it. You got to make snowmen (or was it snow-persons?), have snowball fights, make forts and sometimes even stay home from school. But if you were a grown-up and you had to go somewhere important, the fun could wear a little thin. For adults, snow is something you manufacture and dump on top of hills with chair-lifts and log lodges with roaring fireplaces. Winter and snow should stop wherever it comes into contact with pavement!

But Mother Nature has a long memory and a sense of humour, particularly when it comes to mere human expectations. And every so often she will dust off her old bag of tricks and remind everyone just who is in charge. Then, the only fun part about a good old-fashioned Canadian winter blizzard is reminiscing about how tough it was on the next Canada Day long weekend at the cottage.

A Queen streetcar plows through the remnants of Toronto's worst snow strom, December, 1944.

Commuters lining up for a bus on Yonge Street. Photo: Toronto Sun

Blizzard conditions on King Street near Yonge.

Christmas Eve looking north on Yonge Street in 1924.

High-tech snow removal c.1949.

"Unnatural" is the key word. Winter is not natural. There's a perfectly good reason it is silent out there. Anything with legs or wings and two brain cells to rub together has left - that's why it's silent. Robins, Canada Geese, scarlet tanagers, canaries, monarch butterflies - do you hear them warbling about the eerie, haunting, silent unnatural beauty of a Canadian winter?

Arthur Black, broadcaster

All the man valiantly digging out his car in the photo above can look forward to is joining his fellow commuters on the Don Valley 'Parking Lot' at right. Photos: Toronto Sun

Eglinton Avenue looking east to Kingston Road.

Intersection of Kingston Road and Eglinton looking east, 1952.

KINGSTON ROAD

In 1791, the year John Graves Simcoe was given the responsibility of administering the new Province of Upper Canada (Ontario), he was fully aware that most serious problem facing him was attack by forces from south of the border. Therefore, one of his first acts was to order the construction of a great highway that would connect Kingston to the east – where the military might of the young province was stationed – with a safe site on the Thames River to the west where a new provincial capital would, he thought, be established. Work began on the portion of Simcoe's "great highway" between York (Toronto) and the Thames River in 1793. Seven years later, construction got underway on the York to Kingston hook-up which was completed, albeit with some hard-to-navigate sections, by 1817. In the Scarborough area, the road was blazed through the wilderness by American builder Asa Danforth. Because of hills and other impediments along the way, Danforth chose an inland route that is traced by the modern thoroughfares known as Danforth Road, Painted Post Road, Military Trail and others. The stretch known today as Kingston Road through Scarborough wasn't part of the original trail, but rather started out as a series of small roads connecting farms located close to the lake.

Aerial view looking west from the intersection of Kingston Road and Eglinton Avenue with a city skyline visible in the distance.

SCARBOROUGH BLUFFS

Elizabeth Simcoe, wife of John Graves Simcoe, the province's first lieutenant governor and founder of the City of Toronto, spent much of her early life in Yorkshire in northeastern England. There she was familiar with the seaside town of Scarborough, famed for its soaring cliffs of chalk. The similarity between those cliffs and the ones she discovered a few miles east of the townsite her husband had established prompted Elizabeth to name them the Scarborough Bluffs. Soaring in places to 107 meters (350 feet) above Lake Ontario, the bluffs are a remnant of the last ice age. Approximately 12,000 years ago, the level of the lake reached the top of these bluffs. Then as the ice retreated, the present Lake Ontario took shape and the Scarborough Bluffs remained as a window on thousands of years of pre-history. Erosion of the bluffs and an east-to-west current in the lake led to the formation over eons of time of the sandy peninsula that evolved into today's Toronto Island.

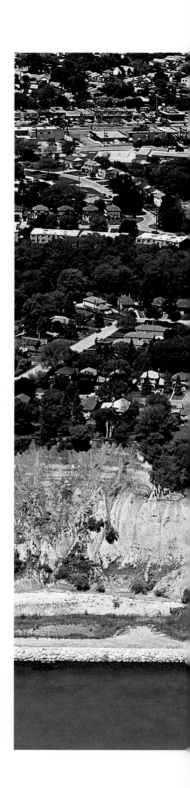

The remarkable Scarborough Bluffs at Midland Avenue and the junction of Kingston Road and Danforth Avenue, 1947. A close look will reveal an isolated house on the top of the bluffs at the foot of Midland Avenue. This house survives in the contemporary photo opposite.

Bluffers Park and its 500-slip marina.

"I like to think that fifteen thousand years ago is only yesterday. And it is. The ice was a mile high on top of Toronto fifteen thousand years ago. That gives me a certain sense of being more at ease in this universe. With that thought behind me, I'm quite sure I'll be able to finish a new book."

Hugh MacLennan 1988

Balmy Beach Club's Silver Birch Boathouse glowing in the reflected light of a beautiful Lake Ontario sunrise.

THE BEACHES

TORONTO BEACHES AREA IS ACTUALLY A COMBINATION OF SEVERAL BEACHES STRETCHING FROM THE SCARBOROUGH BLUFFS EAST TO WOODBINE AVENUE. APART FROM IDYLLIC LAKESIDE VIEWS LIKE THOSE SEEN HERE, THE AREA IS ALSO NOTED FOR THE FUNKY BOHEMIAN OR JUST PLAIN ECCENTRIC SHOPS AND RESTAURANTS THAT LINE QUEEN STREET WHICH PARALLELS THE SHORELINE A COUPLE OF SHORT BLOCKS NORTH. ON A TYPICAL SUMMER EVENING THE ATMOSPHERE IS MORE REMINISCENT OF A NORTHERN RESORT TOWN THAN A NEIGHBOURHOOD JUST A FEW MINUTES FROM THE HEART OF CANADA'S LARGEST CITY. A SIGN OF ITS RESOUNDING POPULARITY IS THE SKYROCKETING REAL ESTATE MARKET AS TORONTONIANS RE-DISCOVER THE AREA. IT IS NOT UNCOMMON FOR HOMES THAT SOLD FOR MERE THOUSANDS IN THE 50S TO COMMAND MILLION DOLLAR PRICE TAGS IN TODAY'S MARKET. BUT THAT IS THE PRICE TO BE PAID FOR BEING ABLE TO LIVE A BLOCK FROM SUNRISES LIKE THIS AND A FIFTEEN MINUTE STREETCAR RIDE TO KING AND BAY.

Three boys up early to experience the magic of a Lake Ontario sunrise.

LEUTY LIFESAVING STATION

The Leuty Lifesaving Station, which was built in 1920 to a design prepared by Toronto architect Alfred Chapman (who would create the CNE's Princes' Gates seven years later) was recently restored at a cost of almost $80,000 of which nearly $70,000 was raised by proud members of the Beach community. This same spirit and sense of community is now being directed to a similar project, the restoration of the 1932 era Beach Boathouse.

THE BOARDWALK

Summer or winter, the neighbourhood population of dogs must be walked and the "Beaches" in this part of Toronto offer as splendid a setting as any to be found in all of Canada for this daily ritual. And with today's renewed interest in health and fitness, the 3 kilometre long boardwalk and bicycle trails that wind along the shoreline play host to strollers, rollerblades and all manner of people-powered modes of transportation.

Spike and block action on Ashbridge's Beach during the annual HEATWAVE Beach Volleyball Tournament.

BEACH VOLLEYBALL

VOLLEYBALL HAS COME A LONG WAY SINCE ITS INTRODUCTION AT A SANTA MONICA, CALIFORNIA PLAYGROUND IN THE EARLY 1920S. THE PLAYING OF THE GAME ON A BEACH TOOK PLACE A FEW YEARS LATER AT A SUBURBAN PARIS, FRANCE NUDIST CAMP. THEN, IN 1947 IT WAS BACK TO CALIFORNIA FOR THE FIRST TWO-MAN BEACH VOLLEYBALL TOURNAMENT. IN 1993, THE SPORT ATTAINED OLYMPIC MEDAL STATUS. THREE YEARS LATER 24 MEN'S AND 16 WOMEN'S TEAMS PARTICIPATED IN THE FIRST EVER OLYMPIC BEACH VOLLEYBALL TOURNAMENT AT THE GAMES IN ATLANTA, GEORGIA.

Despite Toronto's intemperate climate, many of Canada's world class, beach volleyball players grew up in the Beaches area. And Toronto Beaches is the undisputed Mecca for the sport as it plays host to two major beach volleyball events each summer. In June it is the serious business of the Toronto FIVB Pro Tour during which professional players from around the world thrill spectators with their high degree of skill. Then, in July about 300 teams show up for HEATWAVE, an amateur tournament in which proceeds go to Toronto's Hospital for Sick Children.

Site of Old Woodbine race track showing redevelopment already well underway.

WOODBINE

In the fall of 1875, down in the southeast corner of Toronto, not far from the bulrushes and still waters of the ancient Ashbridge's Bay and just a few steps south of the old dirt road to Kingston, two city businessmen, Raymond Pardee and William Howell, stood surveying the large parcel of land they had purchased from Joseph Duggan the previous year. Their plans to build a trotting and racing track were slowly coming to fruition with the first races to be held later that day. It would be called Woodbine Park in honour of the Woodbine Hotel the pair ran at 88 Yonge Street in downtown Toronto.

Race day at Old Woodbine in the 1930s.

The very next year, 1876, Woodbine had achieved sufficient recognition (in spite of several flaws including the fact that the course was frequently flooded) to be designated as the site of that year's running of the Queen's Plate, a prestigious event that had been first contested at the old Carleton Race Course in west Toronto back in 1860. Except for the years 1878-1880, during which the race for the Queen's fifty guineas was held in Prescott, London, Picton and Ottawa respectively, the contest was held at Woodbine Park. This would only change in 1956 when the event was relocated to the new Woodbine track near Toronto (Pearson) International Airport.

Woodbine Park continued as a race course under the name Old Woodbine, a title that was changed once again in 1963 to Greenwood. The end finally came in 1993 when the course was closed and plans unveiled for a major new housing subdivision. In deference to the site's long history, the new streets will bear such names as Sarah Ashbridge Avenue (in honour of one of the area's first settlers), Joseph Duggan Road (named for the person who owned the land on which the original race course was laid out), Glenn Gould Quay (world famous pianist who lived in the nearby Beaches community) and Northern Dancer Boulevard (the most successful thoroughbred in Canadian racing history).

King George VI and Queen Elizabeth attended the King's Plate at Woodbine during their first visit to Canada in 1939. The race winner was Archworth.

197

A recent aerial view of "the Beach" showing, Beaches Park and the boardwalk. The intersection of Wineva and Queen streets is visible in the top left portion of both photos. The entrance into the old park is today's Scarboro Beach Boulevard and can bee seen under the trees to the left of the centre of the photo.

This aerial view of the sprawling Scarboro Beach Amusement Park, at left, was taken in 1925, the park's final year of operation. Developed and opened in 1907 by the Toronto Railway Company (TRC), the city's privately-owned transportation operator, it was what was described as a "trolley park". Access for most visitors was by streetcar during the off-peak hours when the equipment was not in use moving people to and from work. These extra fares plus money generated from the rides, shows and food sales at the park helped add to the TRC's financial bottom line.

Today, Kew Gardens with its adjacent beach and the nearby Woodbine Beach and Balmy Beach (thus the less historically accurate but more descriptive term "the Beaches") have, collectively, become the most popular year-round destination in the entire city.

Torontonians dressed in their Sunday best for a visit to Scarboro Beach Park in 1907.

Dress code of the day for regatta in front of the grand old Hanlan's Point Hotel.

Romantic depiction by James Gray of First Nations people cooking on Gibraltar Point as the Queenston steams leisurely past the town of York toward the western gap and Lake Ontario, 1828. The same view today would be obstructed by the man-made islands that have been constructed since that time.

TORONTO ISLAND

"MY FAVOURITE SANDS," WROTE ELIZABETH SIMCOE IN 1793 IN REFERENCE TO THE NINE-KILOMETRE SPIT OF LAND THAT CURVED SOUTHWESTWARD INTO LAKE ONTARIO FROM THE SHORELINE EAST OF TORONTO'S FORT YORK TO FORM A PROTECTIVE SHIELD AGAINST BOTH HUMANS (INVADERS) AND NATURE (THE TEMPESTS OF THE GREAT LAKES). "CANADA'S LIDO," ENTHUSED AMERICAN ESSAYIST AND TRAVEL WRITER CHARLES DUDLEY WARNER THE FOLLOWING CENTURY, COMPARING THE SAME SANDS TO NORTHERN ITALY'S FAMOUS ISLAND RESORT. IT WASN'T LONG BEFORE A STEADY STREAM OF NATURE LOVERS HAD WORN A PERMANENT CARRIAGE PATH — PART OF THE BOARDWALK ON CENTRE ISLAND RETRACES THIS SAME ROUTE — BETWEEN YORK AND THE FARTHEST TIP OF THE "ISLAND OF HIAWATHA," AS THE PENINSULA WAS AFFECTIONATELY KNOWN.

Appreciated for centuries by the native population as a sacred place of self-rejuvenation, the peninsula itself was constantly being renewed as currents deposited material eroded from the majestic Scarborough Bluffs. Even as it was being built, however, it was also being destroyed, the sandy shoreline shifting with every storm. Finally, on April 13, 1858, it was abruptly and permanently severed from the mainland by a powerful storm which washed away the connecting isthmus, instantly creating Toronto Island. Then, just four days before the confederation of the provinces of Ontario, Quebec, New Brunswick and Nova Scotia into the new Dominion of Canada on July 1, 1867, ownership of the island was transferred to the City of Toronto.

Aerial view of Toronto looking northwest over the Island and Toronto's lovely harbour.

*"When history looks at our city, I have but one wish,
that it will see the greening of Toronto and say:
There, there is where it turned."*

David Crombie 1974
Toronto Mayor in his inaugural address.

The value of this fragile grassy archipelago to urban residents was quickly acknowledged. As early as 1885, city crews began carting landfill and fertilizer to the Island and within two years its sandy mounds had been transformed into a "beautifully landscaped oasis of public resort." Today, the Island – actually a series of possibly 15 islands (there are arguments as to the exact number) – offers a several-hundred-acre (there are arguments about the size as well), car-free (no arguments there!) playground of sandy beaches, limpid lagoons and protected islet wildlife sanctuaries as well as family sports facilities, marinas and trails for hiking and biking.

Today, the only way to reach this paradise is by a ten-minute ferry boat ride. The first privately-owned ferry operation, Michael O'Connor's Horse Boat in 1833, was soon augmented by many others. Before long a problem arose. While vessels from any number of companies would gladly carry passengers to the island, these same companies would frequently remove their craft from service at the first sign of inclement weather thus leaving day trippers stranded. The situation became intolerable and in 1890 one company, the Toronto Ferry Company was established. Thirty-seven years later the city assumed responsibility for all Island ferry service. Today, the proud fleet consists of the *William Inglis* (built in 1935), the *Sam McBride* (1939), the *Thomas Rennie* (1950), the *Ongiara* (1963) and the flower of the fleet, the 1910 steam-powered, authentically restored *Trillium*. They serve three Island destinations: Ward's Island, Centre Island and Hanlan's Point.

WARD'S ISLAND

The most easterly of the trio of Island terminals, Ward's Island welcomed its first resident in 1830 when fisherman David Ward settled there with his wife and seven children. The family no doubt enjoyed the company of the occasional weekend camper who was eager to exchange the summer heat of the city for the cool overnight island interludes. By the beginning of the 20th century, however, there were so many campers that it became necessary to lay out streets in order to bring some semblance of order to the popular get-away spot and then the canvas city began to achieve permanence with the erection of small wooden tent extensions. Pretty soon, a substantial year-round community had taken hold. Today, Ward's Island remains a proud residential community of 650 individuals living in 262 houses whose future is assured under the terms of the Toronto Island Residential Community Trust. And there's an extensive waiting list of more than 500 people hoping to join them, no doubt all of them eager to have as the backdrop to their homes the most spectacular panoramic view possible of Toronto's dynamic downtown skyline.

HANLAN'S POINT

The most westerly of the Island ferry terminals, Hanlan's Point produced Canada's very first world champion athlete. Ned Hanlan was only seven years of age when his father, John, brought his family to settle on the point sometime in the mid-1860s. Surrounded by water for most of his life, it's small wonder that Ned grew up to capture the Canadian, American, British and World sculling championships. And one can't help but conclude that he often rowed past Toronto's oldest landmark, the Gibraltar Point Lighthouse – the oldest existing lighthouse on the Great Lakes, erected on the Island c.1808 and infamous as the site of Toronto's first unsolved murder when lighthouse keeper J.P. Rademuller was killed for a few kegs of beer on January 2, 1815.

Once the setting for picnic groves, dance halls, hotels, several progressively larger baseball stadiums and a popular amusement park complete with "The Big Scream" roller-coaster built in 1894, Hanlan's Point was the ideal site for numerous summer cottages but the opening of the new Sunnyside Amusement Park in 1922 combined with the relocation of the stadium back to the mainland in 1926 triggered a decline in the popularity of the Point. Then, when officials decided in 1937 to locate Toronto's first major airport at this end of the Island, many of the cottages were hauled eastward over the frozen waters of Toronto Bay to a new site on Sunfish Island, now Algonquin Island.

Residents commuting to work from Ward's Island on a rainy fall morning aboard the ferry Ongiara.

Gibraltar Point Lighthouse

Toronto from Centre Island, 1924
Owen Staples (1866-1949)
Oil on board, 21.7 x 26.7 cm.
City of Toronto Art Collection

The city skyline from Centre Island, c.1935

Thirty years later the skyline has changed little as the Royal York Hotel and Bank of Commerce building, hailed as the tallest in the British Commonwealth upon its completion in 1930, still dominate.

CENTRE ISLAND

The busiest of the ferry destinations, Centre Island was a bustling community in the latter part of the 19th century, dotted with the palatial summer homes of many of Toronto's rich and famous. When they eventually moved to the newly developed northern playgrounds of Muskoka and Haliburton, many of their mansions were turned into rooming houses and later, when housing on the mainland became scarce following World War II, apartment houses. This huge influx of new island residents spawned an assortment of shops and stores, a movie house and some restaurants, all thriving until the day in 1953 when the decision was made by City Council to turn the archipelago into public parkland. Before long, wrecking crews had made short work of the Centre Island homes. A variety of trees, shrubs, flower beds and fountains quickly replaced the living, breathing community, to be joined later by an amusement park, a petting zoo, train rides, water slides and many other family diversions. The fact that Centre Island is enjoyed today by over one-and-a-quarter million visitors every year helps to counterbalance the loss suffered by those who used to call it home.

Winter morning on Manitou Road in 1952.

The Island has always been a favourite place for the annual summer picnic and the obligatory portrait.

THE ROYAL CANADIAN YACHT CLUB

THE ROYAL CANADIAN YACHT CLUB WAS FOUNDED IN 1852, INITIALLY UNDER THE TITLE TORONTO BOAT CLUB. IT WAS OPERATED IN THE BRITISH TRADITION OF A RECREATIONAL YACHTING CLUB THAT WOULD UNOFFICIALLY SERVE AS AN AUXILIARY TO THE NAVY. IN 1854, CLUB OFFICIALS SENT A NOTE TO QUEEN VICTORIA ASKING THAT SHE APPROVE HAVING THE WORD "ROYAL" ADDED TO THE NAME MAKING IT THE ROYAL TORONTO BOAT CLUB. A RESPONSE EVENTUALLY ARRIVED INDICATING THAT THE QUEEN HAD GRACIOUSLY APPROVED THE TITLE BE ALTERED TO THE ROYAL CANADIAN YACHT CLUB. THERE WAS NO POINT IN ARGUING THE SLIGHT MANIPULATION OF THE TITLE AND SO ROYAL CANADIAN YACHT CLUB IT WAS.

Though the RCYC is closely associated with Toronto Island, its first clubhouse was actually located on the city's waterfront. The move to the Island didn't occur until 1881. Unfortunately, the organization's first two Island facilities were destroyed by fire, the first in 1904, its successor in 1918. The cornerstone of the present clubhouse was tapped into place by Victoria's great-grandson, Edward, the Prince of Wales on August 25, 1919.

Aerial view showing the Club's perfect location just across the harbour from the big city.

The RCYC's passenger ferry Kwasind was built in 1912. Its running mate Hiawatha is one of the world's oldest operating passenger vessels, launched in 1895. The names of these historic vessels are taken from Henry Wadsworth Longfellow's epic Indian poem which was written in 1855 and in which Hiawatha and Kwasind are good friends.

RCYC from the air, 1925.

The original RCYC clubhouse on the Island was built in 1881. It was destroyed by fire in 1904, a mere 4 months after the heart of the city across the bay also suffered the same fate.

The present RCYC clubhouse was built at a cost of more than half-a-million dollars, quite a sum in 1919.

Members of the RCYC, plus a few hangers-on, pose for this c1901 group photo on the steps of the original Island clubhouse. Of particular interest is the gentleman seated directly behind the bagpiper on the left in the front row. He is Arthur Peuchen, well-travelled Toronto businessman and one-time vice-commodore of the RCYC. Early on the morning of April 15, 1912, his professed skill as a yachtsman got him a seat in RMS Titanic's lifeboat #6. The fact he survived while hundreds of women and children died was to haunt him the rest of his life.

he Queen's Wharf Lighthouse, painted red, stands between the white range light and the lighthouse keeper's residence, just north of the old Western Channel, c.1910.

QUEEN'S WHARF LIGHTHOUSE

Jntil the narrow isthmus that connected the peninsula to the mainland was breached during a fierce storm in 1858, the only access to and from Toronto Bay was through the old Western Channel. It was located almost 400 meters (1,300 feet) north of the present Western Channel, approximately where the busy Lake Shore Boulevard-Bathurst Street intersection is today. The old channel was shallow and awkwardly positioned making it difficult to navigate even under the best weather conditions. To assist boaters, a small lantern was placed at the end of a wooden wharf that jutted into the channel. In 1861, this lantern was replaced by a lighthouse that took the name of the wharf, the Queen's Wharf Lighthouse. This structure stood guard over the old channel until the new Western Channel opened to navigation in 1911. Made obsolete overnight, the old lighthouse was simply abandoned. In 1929, thanks to an unusual (for the time) belief n historic preservation, this ancient monument was moved, using horses and wooden rollers, to its present location where it continues to be maintained by the City of Toronto.

In late 1929, staff of the Toronto Harbour Commission ready the old lighthouse for its move to a new site several hundred meters west of its original location.

The historic lighthouse is now the centrepiece of the Toronto Transit Commission's Lighthouse Loop that was first used in 1931. These two photos were taken in 1936 and 2000.

Above, Peter Witt streetcar dropping passengers at the dock as a ferry captain pulls away, 1929

FERRIES

ONE OF THE OLDEST TRADITIONS IN TORONTO IS THE ROMANTIC JOURNEY BETWEEN THE MAINLAND AND THE ISLAND VIA FERRYBOAT. INDEED, THE ISLAND WAS STILL 35 YEARS AWAY FROM BECOMING AN ISLAND (IT WASN'T SEVERED FROM THE MAINLAND UNTIL A PARTICULARLY VIOLENT STORM OCCURRED IN 1858) WHEN MICHAEL O'CONNOR INTRODUCED THE VERY FIRST FERRY SERVICE. WE KNOW BEYOND A DOUBT THAT HIS FERRYBOAT BOASTED PRECISELY TWO HORSEPOWER BECAUSE ITS PROPULSION EQUIPMENT CONSISTED OF EXACTLY THAT: A PAIR OF HORSES WALKING ON TREADMILLS CONNECTED BY A SERIES OF LEVERS TO SIDEPADDLES THAT DROVE THE LITTLE CRAFT BACK AND FORTH ACROSS THE BAY.

Harbourside view of ferry dock with the new, but still unopened Union Station in the background.

Rising sun bathes the William Inglis and Thomas Rennie in golden light of dawn as crews prepare for another busy day.

As the Island's popularity grew, so too did the number of companies offering cross-bay service – however, their reliability left something to be desired and many a visitor stranded. This situation convinced the city in 1897 to award the service to just one operator, the Toronto Ferry Company, before assuming responsibility itself when insurmountable differences arose 30 years later. Since then, ferry service has been operated by a public body, starting with the Toronto Transportation Commission which added ferry service to its streetcar and bus services in 1927. Throughout the TTC's tenure, the fare was simply two car tickets deposited in a streetcar fare box before boarding the boat – one for the outbound journey, the other to get you home again.

A Toronto Island ferry departs the Centre Island dock.

Sunrise over Toronto Bay silhouettes bow of ferry being prepared for its first sailing of the day.

On January 1, 1962, changes to the municipal structure placed the ferry fleet – the *William Inglis, Sam McBride, Thomas Rennie, Trillium (and one year later) Ongiara* – under the Metropolitan Toronto parks department and then, when the seven local governments of Metro Toronto amalgamated to form the "new" City of Toronto on January 1, 1998, ferry operations became the responsibility of the city's Economic Development, Culture and Tourism Division.

"The question is; if Canadians don't have Toronto to kick around anymore – what in the world will hold this country together?
Not to worry. There's always Ottawa."

Arthur Black, broadcaster.

TRILLIUM

One of the busiest times in the history of the Toronto Island ferry fleet was during the latter years of the 19th century and early years of the 20th when the Toronto Maple Leafs of the International Baseball League played their home games at the old ball stadium at Hanlan's Point. Each summer hundreds of fans would make their way across the bay on one of the Toronto Ferry Company steam-powered ferry boats with the bulk of the work being done by the company's largest vessel, Blue Bell which had entered service in 1906. Over the next few years the baseball Leafs became such a popular attraction that the company found it necessary to add a new boat to the fleet.

Former city mayor David Crombie and a couple of special guests (each of whom was the same age as Trillium) cut the cake at Trillium's 90th birthday party. June 18, 2000.

Launched at the Polson Iron Works yard at the foot of Sherbourne Street on June 18, 1910, the Trillium was quickly fitted out and entered service just in time to transport thousands of fans to the July 1 match at the old Hanlan's Point ball stadium. Trillium remained in service for the next 45 years. Then, with the end of the Second World War, both tire and gas rationing were ended and soon automobiles again became available. These and other factors resulted in a huge drop in the number of people headed for the Island. Soon both Blue Bell and Trillium were simply in the way. The end came in the mid-1950s when both vessels were taken out of service and hidden in an Island lagoon. Their replacements, the more efficient diesel-powered ferry boats, were more than sufficient to handle the dwindling crowds.

In short order, Blue Bell was reduced to a garbage scow and while the same fate was planned for Trillium, for a variety of reasons nothing actually happened. In fact, nothing happened for nearly two decades. Then in 1973, thanks to the efforts of several interested citizens and city politicians, a plan was approved by the members of the Metropolitan Toronto Council that would see the ancient craft rehabilitated and put back into service.

Under the watchful eye of Gordon Champion, the project manager, Trillium's wooden superstructure was replaced (with fireproof aluminum) as was its original Scotch marine boiler (a more efficient package boiler took its place). The double compound steam engine was restored, Trillium's sidepaddles and jennynettles rebuilt and safety equipment added. On November 7, 1975, exactly 23 months after being rescued from that murky Island lagoon, Trillium was back in Toronto Harbour awaiting her future as the flower of the Toronto Island ferry fleet. Trillium's first charter trip took place on May 19, 1976. Since then, thousands have scanned the city's modern, ever changing skyline from the deck of this steam-powered artifact from a bygone era.

Trillium returns from her forced confinement in an Island lagoon as work begins on restoring the historic vessel in 1973.

The steam-powered Trillium sharing a sunny harbour with a sailboat (above) and taking a watery salute from fireboat Wm. Lyon Mackenzie (below) during her 90th birthday celebrations.

MIKE FILEY *came by his love of Toronto's history at a very early age, relying on the city's streetcars to get him to the Bathurst and St. Clair Branch of the public library. And he relied on his parents advice that, should he get lost, just tell the nice policeman your phone number; Melrose 2154. He also remembers a horse trough at the Bathurst/Bloor corner, nor far from where some guy named Mirvish had just moved into the neighbourhood, opening a new store. Then there was his introduction to real poetry at the Downeyflake donut shop where he memorized:*

> *"As you go through life brother,*
> *Whatever be your goal,*
> *Keep your eye upon the donut,*
> *And not upon the hole."*

For the past couple of decades Mike's main focus has been his passion for researching and recording the fascinating history of his hometown. In the process he has written more than a dozen books on various facets of Toronto's past and, for a quarter of a century, has contributed a popular column, "The Way We Were" to the Toronto Sunday Sun newspaper. As a speaker and tour guide on his favourite subject, he is much in demand by local organizations and groups visiting his city.

The Fileys, Mike and wife Yarmila, live, cut grass, shovel snow and pay taxes in Willowdale.

I'd like to thank Julie Kirsh and her helpful staff at the Toronto Sun News Research Centre, friend and computer whiz Jeff Rickard, Fort York's knowledgeable Dr. Carl Benn and my wife Yarmila who, after nearly four decades, continues to be my most enthusiastic booster.

ROSALIND TOSH *wasn't supposed to be an author, but then neither was she supposed to be an historian, a Canadian nor a Sagittarian. However, the sign of the archer claimed her, ready or not, some five decades ago in Ireland and a quarter of a century later, thwarted in love, she herself claimed Toronto as a place of refuge and Canada quickly became the home of her heart, made complete by her husband and two children. The seductive power of historic research was also an unexpected experience for her, reluctantly undertaken some years ago as a favour to a friend and then captivating her as it breathed soul and life into the bricks and mortar and the places and personalities of her beloved New World.*

It was another friend's temporary misfortune 20 years ago that thrust her by chance from the peripherals of high technology into her destiny as a writer. His sickbed plea for someone to replace him as the editor of an Ottawa community newspaper just couldn't be denied and, to her joy and amazement, she discovered that her voice flowed most fluently through the pen. She has been writing ever since.

JOHN MCQUARRIE *is an Ottawa photographer whose major clients include Coors, Marlboro, McDonnell Douglas and Lockheed, but his real passion is producing coffee table books.*

His earlier works focussed on the Canadian Air Force from World War II to the Gulf War, and the Canadian Armed Forces in their roll as Peacekepers. John then turned his lens on the cattle business and working cowboys. And he is quick to point out that his unfulfilled childhood dream of becoming either a cowboy or a fighter pilot has, in later life, finally been realized through the lens of his camera.

The first two titles in his highly acclaimed "Then & Now" series; Above Canada Then & Now and Ottawa Then & Now were released in the Fall of 1999. Future books in this series will include similar treatments for Vancouver, Montreal, Winnipeg, Halifax and New York.

He also intends to produce a photographic portrait of Scotland's single malt whisky industry and another on Canada's fisheries.

The people of Toronto are very fortunate to have a variety of resources that safeguard and showcase the rich pictorial history of this wonderful city. But these vast resources would be impossible to access without the knowledgeable and cheerful research staff that make the task of finding archival images so enjoyable and productive. The people who led this publisher to the treasures within these pages are gratefully acknowledged here.

Christine Bourolias, Mary Ledwell and James Bowers
Archives of Ontario
Andrea Aitken, Mark Cuddy, John Huzil, Glenda Williams and Lincoln Ross
City of Toronto Archives
Pamela Wachna
Coordinator of Collections and Outreach, Culture Division, City of Toronto
The Mike Filey Collection

Archives of Ontario: Page 61, 90 both, 92 bottom left and bottom right, 93 bottom left and bottom right, 103, 106 top, 110, 111 top, 113 bottom left and bottom right, 115, 157 all, 158, 160, 162 bottom right, 163 bottom right, 165 top left, 167 bottom left and bottom right, 169 bottom left, 180 top left and top right, 184, 186, 209 top left.

City of Toronto Archives: Page 58 (10090), 87 (1220), 120 top left (1008), 155 top (1568), 156 (79), 170 (777F), 171 top (821), 176 bottom right (TTC 3376), 177 (TTC 50014), 200 (162), 201 (163).